JERROLD G JEFFERSON
HCR 1 BOX 7040
IGO CA 96047

SO-CYE-549

JULIE MENENDEZ is professor of Physical Education and Soccer Coach at San Jose State College. He is a member of the National Collegiate Athletic Association's Soccer Rules and Tournament Committee and the United States Olympic Soccer Committee, and is Chairman of the Far West Intercollegiate All-American Soccer Committee. Professor Menendez is President of the West Coast Intercollegiate Soccer Conference and a Senior Staff Coach for the California Soccer Football Association.

MATT BOXER, President of the Northern California Soccer Football Association, was elected to the United States Soccer Football Association's National Hall of Fame in 1961 for his contributions to the sport as player, coach, and administrator. He is currently District Commissioner for the United States Soccer Football Association and has served as President of the California Soccer Football Association. Mr. Boxer has been active for over forty years in organizing and promoting soccer, both in the United States and abroad.

SOCCER

JULIE MENENDEZ
SAN JOSE STATE COLLEGE

MATT BOXER
NATIONAL SOCCER HALL OF FAME

Foreword by
WILSON T. HOBSON, JR.
UNITED STATES OLYMPIC COMMITTEE
TREASURER, UNITED STATES SOCCER FOOTBALL ASSOCIATION

THE RONALD PRESS COMPANY • NEW YORK

Copyright © 1968 by
THE RONALD PRESS COMPANY

All Rights Reserved

No part of this book may be reproduced
in any form without permission in writing
from the publisher.

Library of Congress Catalog Card Number: 68–8625
PRINTED IN THE UNITED STATES OF AMERICA

Foreword

This book arrives on the scene at a most auspicious time—when soccer, the world's most popular sport, is beginning to enjoy a wave of popularity in the United States.

I am especially pleased to see our youth taking up the game as early as at the age of eight. Since throughout the world children generally begin playing soccer at this age—or even younger—our players have traditionally been as much as six to eight years behind those of other countries in developing the basic skills of soccer. Fortunately, this gap is beginning to narrow.

As soccer programs develop and expand, this book will prove an asset and guide to coaches, players of all age groups, and spectators. This volume is profusely illustrated and presents the skills, training techniques, and strategy of soccer football in a comprehensive and precise manner. This is a book designed to make unique contributions to the game in the United States.

It has been a pleasure to be associated with Julie Menendez in the Olympic and Development programs and Matt Boxer in the United States Soccer Football Association. They are both dedicated to the development of soccer in the United States and their interest knows no bounds.

WILSON T. HOBSON, JR.

Chairman, Soccer Football Committee of the United States Olympic Committee;

Treasurer, United States Soccer Football Association

Preface

For the first time in history the national sport of more than 125 countries is on the threshold of attaining in the United States the status and recognition it enjoys throughout the rest of the world. Soccer is British in origin and in the United States was long regarded as a foreign game to be played by foreigners. The turning point came, perhaps, when Americans recognized the value of the sport and realized that it should be treated as a universal game to be played by Americans in a world community of sport.

This book is designed to meet the need for a synthesis of information about soccer as it relates to the American scene. For coaches it offers teaching plan and aids, training programs, and comprehensive discussions of offensive and defensive strategy. Players are provided with complete, clearly illustrated coverage of all the fundamental skills, and explanations of the techniques and responsibilities of the individual playing positions. For those charged with introducing or expanding soccer programs in schools, clubs, or recreation departments, there are detailed descriptions of facilities and equipment, and advice on the administration of tournaments and clinics. Parents and spectators interested in increasing their understanding and enjoyment of the game will find here a useful introduction to the objectives and philosophy of soccer.

From time to time, reference is made to soccer programs in other countries in the hope that their valuable features may be adapted to similar programs in the United States.

The authors wish to express their appreciation to Jess Logan, who prepared the illustrations; to Major Raoul Mollet, Secretary–Treasurer of the International Military Sports Council (CISM), Brussels, for permission to include his material on power training for soccer; to Dr. Charles Lynn Walker, San Jose State College, for his helpful suggestions toward improvement of the manuscript; to John Sherry, Photographer, San Francisco; and to others acknowledged in the text who provided valuable materials.

JULIE MENENDEZ
MATT BOXER

San Jose, California
San Francisco, California
July, 1968

Contents

APPENDIXES

Key to Diagrams

 = OPPOSING PLAYERS

 = MOVEMENT OF PLAYER WHO HAS CHANGED POSITION

 = KICK OR THROW

 = DRIBBLE

———————————▶ = MOVEMENT OF PLAYER WITHOUT BALL

 = FEINT

1. (G) = GOALKEEPER
2. (RB) = RIGHT-FULLBACK
3. (CH) = CENTER-HALFBACK
4. (LB) = LEFT-FULLBACK
5. (RH) = RIGHT-HALFBACK
6. (LH) = LEFT-HALFBACK
7. (RW)-(OR) = RIGHT-WING OR OUTSIDE-RIGHT
8. (IR) = INSIDE-RIGHT
9. (CF) = CENTER-FORWARD
10. (IL) = INSIDE-LEFT
11. (LW)-(OL) = LEFT-WING OR OUTSIDE-LEFT

SOCCER

1

Soccer in the United States

Soccer was first introduced into the United States in the 1870's. Most of the early games were played in haphazard fashion by Scotch, Irish, and English immigrants who settled along the eastern seaboard. Gradually, the sport moved westward to Detroit, Cincinnati, Cleveland, Chicago, St. Louis, Denver, and the Far West. In the beginning, interest in the sport was usually confined to the foreign immigrants who settled in these areas. Frank G. Menke reported in his encyclopedia of sports: "The growth of soccer in this country, as compared to other nations, has been slow, chiefly because it was erroneously felt that it lacked that combative element that the American public has come to consider as an essential part of sport. However, interest in the game for the game's sake has been increasing rapidly in recent years. It is one sport adapted for international competition."[1] It was the international appeal of the sport that led to its American growth because the game held a universal language for the millions who migrated to this country, before and after World War I.

Soccer continued a slow but steady growth through the early 1900's. As the game began to take a firm hold, regional and local governing bodies came into existence. (See Appendix for outlets for United States soccer.)

In December, 1927, the College Physical Education Association appointed a committee on Curriculum Research to formulate a basic program of physical education for the schools of America. Soccer was one of the activities recommended by the committee for basic physical education programs in elementary, junior, and senior high schools. The committee used the following criteria in evaluating the several activities:

[1] Frank G. Menke, *The Encyclopedia of Sports* (New York: A. S. Barnes and Company), 1960.

3

1. The contribution to the *physical* and *organic* growth and development of the child and the improvement of body function and body stability.
2. The contribution to the *social traits* and qualities that go to make up the good citizen and the development of sound moral ideals through intensive participation under proper leadership.
3. The contribution to the *psychological* development of the child including satisfactions resulting from stimulating experiences physically and socially.
4. The contribution to the development of *safety* skills that increase the individual's capacity for protection in emergencies, both in handling himself and in assisting others.
5. The contribution to the development of *recreational skills* that have a distinct function as hobbies for leisure time hours, both during school and after school life.[2]

In spite of the committee's recommendation, the majority of the American schools failed to include soccer in their sports programs. As a result many American boys are still being denied the opportunity to participate in a worthwhile activity which embodies the finest qualities found in sport. This is one of the reasons for the low ranking of the United States in Olympic and other international soccer competitions. In the rest of the world, the average boy is as skilled in soccer by the time he reaches high school as the average boy in the United States is in baseball or basketball.

In some instances the absence of soccer programs is due to a lack of understanding of the sport. If soccer is to achieve the same status as other sports commonly taught and played in American schools, the nature and purpose of the game must be understood. Therefore, this chapter has a twofold purpose: to provide information that helps answer questions regarding the sport; and to provide information that will assist in initiating new programs.

PERSONAL VALUES FOR PARTICIPANTS

"Soccer-Football is a sport that can be played with equal benefit and pleasure from the ages of six to forty and above." [3] Sir Stanley Matthews, renowned British player, was an international star well into his forties. Once played the game appeals to American youth.

[2] W. Ralph LaPorte, *The Physical Education Curriculum* (Los Angeles: The University of Southern California Press), 1947, p. 7.
[3] Leo Weinstein, "The Physical Fitness Puzzle: A Call for Action" (unpublished article, Stanford, California, 1961).

Soccer appeals to all ages.

A recent study, on the status of soccer at colleges and universities in the United States, reveals that students take the greatest share in originating soccer programs.[4]

The sport appeals to participants for various reasons:

1. It is a sport in which size is not a factor because it does not require unusual height or weight. An equal chance for all students is one of the inherent values of the sport.
2. It requires a minimum of equipment.
3. It promotes physical fitness because endurance and speed play important roles in the game.
4. It enables all the players to learn scientific skills with movements which are constant and spontaneous.
5. It promotes co-operation and teamwork because all the players must combine their talents to achieve success.

[4] Hans Gunther Buhrmann, "The Status of Soccer at Colleges and Universities in the United States" (unpublished thesis, George Williams College, Chicago, 1963).

6. In a world shrinking in size, soccer-football is and has been a good link between people of different traditions. The World Cup Tournament points up the universal language of the game.

7. The rules of the game are simple.

8. The strategy of the game involves a scientific approach which can be readily understood.

9. It creates mental situations which call for split-second decisions and constructive patterns.

10. The sport is dynamic in character.

INJURIES

Soccer is a rugged but relatively safe activity. Injuries of a serious nature do not often occur in the game of soccer. An estimated 250 million players participate in the game annually on a world-wide basis, and the injury rate is extremely low. However, there are elements of danger in all sports and although injuries are minor in soccer, they do occurr and must be considered.

A prerequisite for any endurance-type activity is a physical examination by a doctor followed by a training program that will condition a player for the sport. The parts of the body most susceptible to injuries are the legs and the ankles. Injuries to the legs usually involve pulled muscles. Shin guards will help minimize the chance of injury to the legs and players with weak ankles are encouraged to tape them for support.

A strict observance of the rules by coaches and officials will also reduce the risk of injury. The laws of the game permit shoulder-to-shoulder contact when two players are contesting for the ball; however, the contact must be incidental to ball play. The philosophy and object of the game is to "play the ball—not the man." The rules treat dangerous play situations as infractions and give the referee the right to exercise his discretion in determining whether or not a play or a player's action is of such nature as to be dangerous or likely to cause injury. Rules covering dangerous play situations are covered in detail by the rule book of The United States Soccer Football Association and The Official Collegiate–Scholastic Soccer Guide.

SOCCER AND PHYSICAL FITNESS

When considering what kind of sports are needed to induce people to participate and to improve their physical condition, Dr. Leo Weinstein, former Stanford University soccer coach, cites the following prerequisites: "It should be of such nature as to permit constant participation by all who are playing; it should stress endurance and develop the entire body; its rules should be simple; it should require low-cost and lasting equipment; it should be a sport that can be played all year round; it should not require unusual physical height or weight." [5]

Soccer meets all of the above-mentioned qualifications. When properly conducted, it is an endurance-type activity which lends itself well to physical fitness. After seeing his first soccer match, the late William Leiser remarked: "In requirement of physical condition this is the toughest game we have ever observed. You do this and you do that, in rapid succession, but always in between you run and you run and you run again, maybe 100 yards or more at a time, for 45 minutes. You rest ten, then you run 45 minutes again. Only the goalkeeper can take it easy between plays like American footballers do or like baseballers shifting innings." [6] The pattern of play calls for constant motion and utilizes sprints, jogging, and walking. Actually, soccer requires "interval training" under competitive conditions. In addition, it accommodates large groups in an organized activity. It is an ideal activity for a physical education program.

SPECTATOR APPEAL

Soccer appeals to the spectators because it is an exciting sport that is easy to understand. Leiser summed up the reaction most fans experience when they are first exposed to a soccer match:

We understood why as we watched the first game of soccer we ever saw, Sunday at Balboa Stadium when Peru's champs were against what we were told was an exceptional team of San Francisco all stars. The reasons are many, but we'll cite two:

First, anybody can follow the game first time he looks at it. A man who doesn't know can look at American baseball, for instance, or at British cricket, and never know from "nuthin" for weeks, even if an expert is explaining to him. Watch soccer and you get the idea quick, you understand, and you can pick up rules and fine points later.

Second, any fan can immediately appreciate the vast variety of skills required to play soccer well, from speed afoot to body balance, delicate control, kicking and heading accuracy and awareness of position of teammates at all times. It's perhaps the greatest of games this soccer, even if we are the last to discover it. [7]

[5] Weinstein, *op. cit.*, p. 1.

[6] William Leiser, "The Best Game of Them All," *San Francisco Chronicle,* March 7, 1962.

[7] *Ibid.,* p. 25.

SOCCER AND OTHER KICK-TYPE ACTIVITIES

In some quarters it is felt that soccer's growth in the United States has been affected by the impression that soccer and American football are similar; that the addition of soccer to the program would create a conflict of interest for teachers, coaches, athletes, and spectators. This unfounded fear stems from the fact that soccer-football is the parent game of rugby, which in turn is the parent game of American football. Unfortunately, American football adopted the name football, which is the name soccer answers to in almost every country throughout the world. American football has developed into a unique game where the object of the game is to use the hands rather than the feet. In soccer the opposite holds true: kicking is the chief skill to be learned. American soccer and American football are two different games, and they should not be confused.

On occasion, the game of soccer is misrepresented by other kick-type activities. Lead-up games are important; however, as soon as possible, the game of soccer should be played according to the rules. Playing according to the rules does not rule out the practice of modifying the players' equipment, size of field, and the duration of the game to meet the needs and abilities of age-group soccer. Nor does it imply an attempt to overemphasize the game. American interscholastic and intercollegiate soccer is free of the pressure and commercialized trends which have become associated with many sports. Overemphasis is not a problem which is likely to develop to the point where it will detract from the educational values of the activity.

American youngsters like to emulate the outstanding stars whose names appear on the sports page; soccer has its heroes and this is a motivating force behind the sport. This has also been a factor in stimulating growth and interest in other sports, namely: baseball, football, track and field, boxing, swimming, etc.

Soccer is a game which can be played the year round. If properly scheduled, it can complement a school's physical education, intramural, and athletic programs. Many high schools in the United States are scheduling their soccer programs after the conclusion of the American football season and before the beginning of the spring sports season. For sections of the United States where the weather is not too severe, this is the logical time for soccer to be added to the program, as this constitutes the indoor season in most athletic programs. As a rule, basketball, swimming, and wrestling are also scheduled at this time of the year; however, they are usually limited as to the number of students who may participate.

The adoption of soccer by the American sports scene is in keeping with the manner in which this country has adopted and perfected other sports originally considered foreign, namely: golf, tennis, gymnastics, swimming, water polo, etc.

2

Getting Started

The requirements needed to get a soccer program started are briefly described here: selecting a coach, and securing facilities, game and personal equipment, and knowledge of the basic rules.

SELECTING A COACH

Ideally, a soccer coach for a school program should be a trained physical educator with an interest and background in the sport. If such a person is not immediately available, use an in-service training program to develop the quality of instruction and coaching needed for the assignment. Whenever possible, involve other instructors in the school who have a background and interest in the game.

The good coach, trainer, or teacher of soccer should:

1. Know the sport—its rules and requirements.
2. Be well versed in the fundamentals of the sport.
3. Be well versed in the training techniques required to condition athletes for an endurance-type activity.
4. Supervise all workouts.
5. Demand a strict observance of the rules by his players.
6. Have a keen sense of sportsmanship and fair play.

FACILITIES

The term facilities applies to space, structures, and equipment needed for a soccer program. Actually, soccer demands less in the way of facilities than the majority of sports. The essential requirement is a level turfed area suitable for marking off a soccer field. The majority of schools in the United States have turfed areas suitable for soccer. On the high school and college levels, whenever possible, use existing stadium facilities for day or night soccer.

Besides allowing for greater use of school facilities, it will increase player and spectator interest in the sport. The conversion of a football field into a soccer facility (and its reconversion) requires few changes and a minimum amount of work. To convert a football field into a soccer facility, place portable soccer goals in front of the existing football goals and increase the width of the field by five yards on each side. This will provide a playing area well within the rules of the game.

MARKING THE FIELD

The soccer field is rectangular in shape, not less than 100 yards or more than 130 yards in length and no less than 50 yards or more than 100 yards in width. The *touch lines* are the lines marking the length boundaries of the field. The *goal lines* are the lines at each end of the field, joining and at right angles to the touch lines.

To lay out the field of play, mark the boundaries of the field with distinctive lines, not more than five inches and not less than one and one-half inches in width. Place the goals on the center of each goal line so that the goal posts are equidistant from the corner flags and eight yards apart (inside measurement). Mark a *half-way line* across the field of play and a *center circle* with a ten yard radius at the center of the field.

Mark the *goal area* at each end of the field by extending two lines from the goal line, at a point six yards from each goal post, onto the field of play for a distance of six yards, and join the two lines by drawing a line parallel with the goal line. The distance along this parallel line should measure 20 yards = 60 feet.

To mark the *penalty area* at each end of the field draw two lines at right angles to the goal line, 18 yards from each goal post and extend them onto the field of play for a distance of 18 yards. Join the two lines by drawing a line parallel with the goal line. The distance along this parallel line should measure 44 yards = 132 feet. (See Fig. 2–1.) Inside each penalty area, mark the *penalty spot*, 12 yards from the mid-point of the goal line. From each penalty spot, mark an arc of a circle outside the penalty area. The radius of the *penalty arc* is 10 yards from the penalty spot.

Mark the *corner areas* by drawing inside the field of play a quarter circle with a radius of one yard. (See Fig. 2–2.) The rules call for a flag in each corner of the field. In addition, optional flags may be placed not less than three feet outside the touch lines to mark the mid-field line. Use five-foot rounded posts with colored bunting for the corner flags. Regulation flag poles are available at most outlets for soccer equipment, or can be made locally.

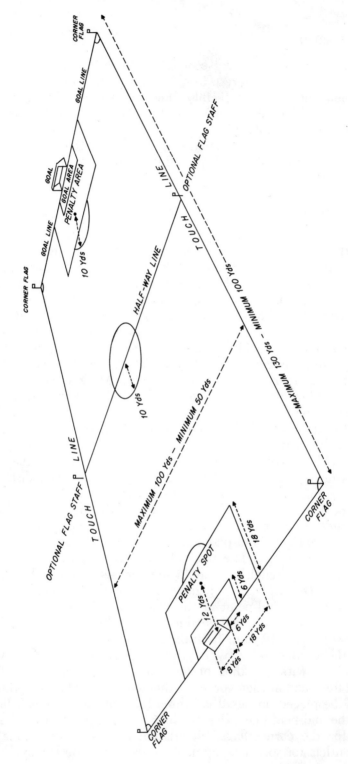

Fig. 2-1. Field of play.

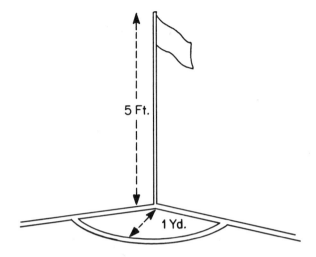

Fig. 2–2.   Mark the corner areas.

THE GOALS

A soccer goal (Fig. 2–3) consists of two upright posts, a horizontal cross-bar, and attachments for hanging a net in back of and behind the goal. The measurements of the goal are eight yards between the insides of the two uprights and eight feet from the ground to the lower edge of the cross-bar. The laws of the game state that the width and depth of the goal posts and the width and depth of the cross-bar shall not exceed five inches. For permanent goal fixtures, sink the uprights 18 to 24 inches into the ground and set them in concrete.

To construct portable goals, weld two-inch pipe into a goal frame. Support the frame by welding a five-foot length of two-inch pipe to the base and rear of each upright, along with a one-inch metal rod from the top and rear of each upright. Shape the rods so that the net will drape in back of and down behind the goal. Join the two back ends of the base supports and the bottom ends of the metal rods with a two-inch pipe running parallel to the goal line. Make an allowance for the insertion of wheels into sleeves in the corners of the goal. For the attachment of the goal net, weld small hooks ten to twelve inches apart, on the back of the uprights and cross-bar. As a safety measure, use 2 × 4 inch boards with rounded edges to face the goals. Clamp the boards to the pipe forming the face of the goal and paint them white.

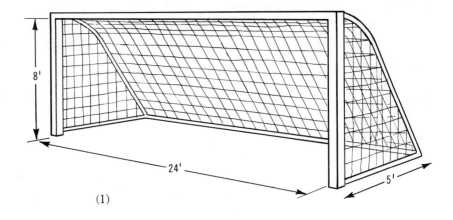

(1)

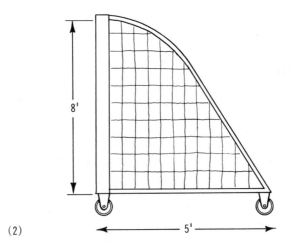

(2)

Fig. 2–3.   Soccer goal.

1. Goal measurements.
2. Use detachable wheels.

BOUNDING BOARD

A goal-size bounding board (Fig. 2–4) which can be used on both sides, is a valuable adjunct to a soccer training program. The bounding board allows for continuous repetition of kicking, passing, and ball control drills. It is an excellent learning and conditioning device.

To construct a bounding board, sink seven 4 × 4 inch posts 18 to 24 inches into the ground and set them in concrete. To stay with the proper goal dimensions, keep the posts four feet apart and make allowance for a height of eight feet from the surface of the ground. Nail eight 2 × 12 inch planks across both sides of the posts and one 2 × 8 inch plank across the top of the bounding board.

As an aid to perfecting low shots into the corners of the goal, paint targets at the lower corners of both sides of the board. Allow for a margin of at least 18 inches from the edge of the bounding board to the target.

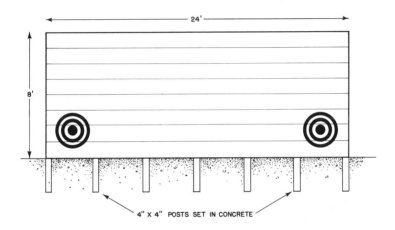

Fig. 2–4. Bounding board.

SUSPENDED-BALL APPARATUS

A free-swinging suspended ball is a valuable aid for teaching and learning heading, kicking, and various techniques associated with goal tending. In addition, it can play an important role in training for soccer. (See "Power Training," in Chapter 4.)

To construct an indoor suspended-ball apparatus (Fig. 2–5), bolt a five-foot metal arm to a wall, at a height of 12 to 13 feet. Attach a small pulley at the end of the arm next to the wall, and weld a small hook with a ball-bearing swivel at the other end. Thread a nylon cord through the pulley and hook and attach it to a tether ball, or to a soccer ball that has been fitted with a special loop attachment.

Fig. 2–5.   Suspended-ball assembly.

Adjust the height of the suspended ball to suit each individual player.   Anchor the cord and store excess line to an attachment on the wall.

For an outdoor apparatus, bolt the arm to a metal pole and follow the same specifications.

GAME AND PERSONAL EQUIPMENT

See the Appendix for a soccer checklist covering game equipment.

THE SOCCER BALL

The laws of the game state that the ball be spherical, the outer casing shall be of leather, and no material shall be used in its construction which might prove dangerous to the players. The circumference of the ball shall not be more than 28 inches nor less than 27 inches.   The weight of the ball at the start of the game shall not be more than 16 ounces nor less than 14 ounces.

There are a variety of soccer balls on the market that meet the rules and specifications of the sport. Recent innovations include plastic-coated soccer balls which ward off moisture and balls designed for night soccer.

PERSONAL EQUIPMENT

A player's equipment consists of a pair of soccer shoes, sweat socks, shin guards, stockings, metal cup supporter, pants, and jersey. For age-group soccer use gym shoes; they are safer, and, in addition, they help young players develop the touch needed to control the ball.

Goalkeepers require some specialized gear, namely: pants with thigh pads, knee pads, jerseys that are different in color from both teams', and gloves that allow for better gripping in wet or cold weather. In addition, a goalkeeper often uses a cap to help shield the sun from his eyes.

RULES AND POSITIONS

Eleven players, including the goalkeeper, comprise each team. A basic formation calls for one goalkeeper, two fullbacks, three halfbacks, and five forwards. The positions are numbered one through eleven, and the players usually wear numbers on the back of their uniforms which correspond to their positions. (See Fig. 2–6.)

DURATION OF GAME

The United States Soccer Football Association abides by the International Rules, which call for two equal periods of 45 minutes with a half-time not to exceed 5 minutes except by consent of the referee. At the Junior level, the duration of the game is 60 minutes divided into 2 equal periods of 30 minutes each.

For the rules governing the duration of the game at the college and high school levels, the reader is referred to the National Intercollegiate Athletic Association Soccer Guide. For age-group soccer, modify the duration of the game, according to the age, physical condition, and ability of the participants.

SCORING

A goal (one point) is scored when the entire ball passes over the goal line, between the posts, and under the cross-bar, provided it is not thrown, carried, or propelled by a hand or arm of an attacking player.

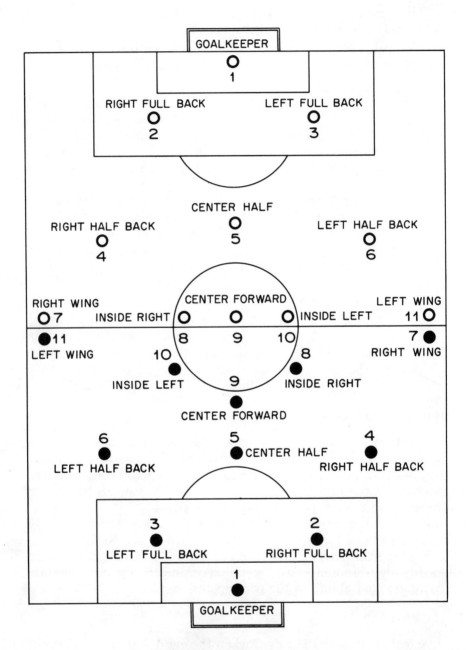

Fig. 2–6. Players' positions.

STARTING THE PLAY

At the beginning of the game, decide choice of ends and the kick-off with the toss of a coin. The team winning the toss has the option of ends or the kick-off.

To start the game, place the ball on the ground in the center of the field. Once the referee gives the signal, the player kicking off must move the ball forward at least the distance of its circumference. The kicker is not permitted to play the ball a second time until it has been touched or played by another player. At the time of the kick-off, every player must be in his own half of the field and every player of the team opposing that of the kicker must remain not less than ten yards from the ball until it is kicked off. Use the same method to restart the game after a goal has been scored. The kick-off goes to the team losing the goal. When starting the second half of the game, the teams change ends and the kick-off is taken by a player of the opposite team to that of the player who started the game.

OUT-OF-BOUNDS

The ball is out of play when it completely crosses the goal line or touch line, whether on the ground or in the air. The three methods of putting a ball back in play after it has gone out-of-bounds are: 1) *Throw-in:* At the point where the ball goes over the sideline, the team opposite that which touched it last receives a throw-in. 2) *Goal kick:* When the attackers last touch a ball going over the goal line (endline), the defenders are awarded a goal kick. The ball is placed on the ground and kicked from the goal area. 3) *Corner kick:* When the whole of the ball passes over the goal line, excluding that portion between the goal posts and under the cross-bar, either in the air or on the ground, having last been played by one of the defending team, a member of the attacking team takes a kick from within the quarter-circle at the nearest corner. A goal may be scored direct from a corner kick. In a corner kick situation, players of the opposing team are not permitted within ten yards of the ball until it is in play, e.g., it has travelled the distance of its own circumference. The kicker is not permitted to play the ball a second time until it has been touched or played by another player.

Free kicks are awarded as the result of fouls. No foul is called unless it is intentional and, in all cases, the referee is the sole judge. A *direct free kick* is a situation during which a goal may be scored directly and the kick is awarded at the spot of the foul for the following violations: tripping, kicking, holding, striking, pushing, charging violently, jumping at an opponent, or handling the ball.

If these violations are committed by a defender within his penalty area, the attacking team is given a *penalty kick* from the penalty spot. When it is being taken, all players, with the exception of the player taking the kick and the opposing goalkeeper, must be within the field of play but outside the penalty area and at least ten yards from the penalty-mark. The defending goalkeeper must stand, without moving his feet, on his own goal line, between the goal posts, until the ball is kicked. A goal may be scored direct from a penalty kick.

Indirect free kicks are awarded for lesser violations and a goal cannot be scored until the ball has been touched by another player. An indirect kick is awarded at the spot of the foul for the following violations: playing in a manner considered by the referee to be dangerous; charging fairly with the shoulder when the ball is not within playing distance of the players concerned; when not playing the ball, intentionally obstructing an opponent; charging the goal-keeper; or when the goalkeeper takes more than four steps while holding the ball without bouncing it on the ground.

OFF-SIDE

An attacker is off-side if there are not at least two defenders be-tween himself and the goal at the moment the ball is played to him. He is not off-side if he is behind the ball; if the ball last touched an opponent; if he is in his half of the field; or if he receives the ball directly from a goal kick, corner kick, throw-in, or when it is dropped by the referee.

3

Soccer Fundamentals

Soccer is a team game in which the main objective is to score by putting the ball into the opponents' goal by playing it with any part of the body except the hands and arms. Skills in kicking, trapping, passing, dribbling, tackling, heading, goal tending, and throwing are the components of soccer technique and are essential to the offensive and defensive tactics of the game.

STEPS IN TEACHING

Use the following sequence to teach soccer fundamentals and to mold soccer technique:

1. *Introduction:* Introduce the skill with a brief explanation of its purpose and importance.
2. *Demonstration:* Provide a correct picture of the skill in the minds of the players by using an expert demonstrator or an instructional technique, such as, a movie, film loop, or sequence diagram to demonstrate the skill.
3. *Explanation:* Explain and analyze the component parts of the skill and relate them to the mental picture implanted in the minds of the players by the demonstration.
4. *Imitation:* Give players, through a series of drills, opportunities to try the skill.
5. *Game Situations:* After the basic form has been learned, it is essential to practice, through a controlled scrimmage, the fundamentals as they relate to the offensive and defensive tactics of the game.
6. *Correction:* Point out and correct individual and team mistakes as soon as they occur. In a controlled scrimmage, stop the action if the correction will benefit the entire team. Whenever practicable, correct individual mistakes.
7. *Repetition:* Repeat drill and game-type situations which will improve skill performance and team proficiency.

8. *Competition:* Schedule a game to give the players an opportunity to perform under pressure. Through competition point out weaknesses, mistakes, and the need for advanced skills and tactics in light of the whole strategy of the sport. Use chalk talks and game experience to emphasize plans of action that depend upon preliminary moves and skill performances by individual players.

KICKING

Kicking the ball is the main skill to be learned in the game of soccer; it is the method most often used to control and to propel the ball towards the opponents' goal.

During a game the ideal kicking situation would permit a player sufficient time to control the ball and to place it at the proper angle for an effective kick. However, the nature of the game does not often allow for ideal kicking situations. Sometimes the ball is rolling or bouncing on the ground and sometimes it is in the air. A player must learn to kick from whatever position he may be, however the ball happens to come to him. The type of kick to be used is determined by the tactical advantage to be served which, in turn, is influenced by the challenge of the opposition and the position of the ball. Different situations call for different kicks. Consequently, a player must master a variety of kicks. The following skills have been refined and are accepted by most authorities as the techniques which constitute the kicking phase of the game.

The type of kick to be used is influenced by many factors. (Photo by Michael Jencks)

Instep kick: plant the non-kicking foot, heel first, alongside the ball. (Photo by Michael Jencks)

INSTEP KICK

The instep kick is used for shots at goal, as well as long and short passes. When shooting it allows for both maximum power and control, as it enables the kicker to meet the ball with a large surface of the foot. The approach run for an instep kick calls for a few short steps and a longer stride when the non-kicking foot is planted near the ball. The short steps help generate power for the kick and the longer stride which just precedes the kick allows for proper timing because it gives the kicking leg the time and space needed to swing into the ball. To execute the instep kick, move to meet the ball, plant the non-kicking foot, heel first, alongside the ball and point it in the direction the ball is to go. The distance of the non-kicking foot from the ball varies with individuals and must be worked out with experience. (See Fig. 3–1.) Swing the kicking foot into ac-

Fig. 3–1. For the instep kick, the distance of the non-kicking foot from the ball varies with individuals.

Fig. 3–2. Keep the knee and the weight of the body over the ball.

tion at the moment the knee and the weight of the body are over the ball. (See Fig. 3–2.) At the moment of impact, clench the toes against the sole of the foot and meet the ball with the instep, or shoe-lance portion of the boot. (See Fig. 3–3.) To get force into a kick, straighten the knee as the foot moves into the ball and swing the leg clean and free by following through after the ball.

To keep a kick low, place the non-kicking foot to the side of the ball, get the knee and weight of the body over the ball, and point the toes of the kicking foot down, at the moment of impact.

To loft a ball high into the air, place the non-kicking foot behind and to the side of the ball, lean the body slightly backward, and reach for the ball with the kicking foot. Meet the ball just below

Fig. 3–3. Kick the ball with the instep.

the mid-point, and point the toes of the kicking foot upward on the follow through.

THE VOLLEY

A volley is a kick when the ball is off the ground. It is used for defensive clearances, in certain passing situations, and for quick shots at goal. A kick is called a full-volley when contact is made with the ball before it hits the ground; it is called a half-volley when the kick is made just as the ball bounces from the ground. The full-volley is usually associated with high clearance kicks while the half-volley is a quick method for executing a hard shot at goal. However, this is not an ironclad rule, as players often have opportunities for shots for goal with the full-volley, and the half-volley may also be used as a clearance kick.

When a long kick or hard shot is desired, use the instep kick to volley the ball. For a short pass, a volley with the inside of the foot can be very effective.

To execute the full-volley, place the non-kicking leg behind and to the side of the ball with the foot pointed in the direction the ball is to travel. With the body leaning slightly backward and the head behind the knee of the kicking foot, meet the ball with an instep kick. Keep the head down, eyes on the ball, and use the arms to help balance the weight of the body over the non-kicking leg. (See Fig. 3–4.) The loft of the ball is controlled by the dis-

Fig. 3–4. The volley.
1. Kick the ball with the instep of the foot.
2. Balance the weight of the body over the non-kicking leg.

tance the player leans back from the ball, the height of the ball, and the angle of the kicking foot at the moment of impact. To keep the full-volley low, get the body and knee of the kicking foot closer to the ball and point the toes of the kicking foot down at the moment of impact.

To execute the half-volley, time the kick so that the instep of the

(1)   (2)

(3)   (4)

Fig. 3–5. The half-volley.

1. Head down, eyes on the ball and the arms out to the sides.
2. Kick the ball just as it rebounds from the ground.
3. Time the kick.
4. Follow through and balance the weight of the body over the non-kicking leg.

kicking foot meets the ball just as it rebounds from the ground. The half-volley requires perfect timing. It is an excellent technique for a quick shot at goal. (See Fig. 3–5.)

(1)   (2)

Fig. 3–6.   Over-head kick.

1. Lean backward and reach for the ball with the kicking leg.
2. Volley the ball back and over the head.

OVER-HEAD KICK

The over-head kick is one of soccer's unorthodox techniques. As a rule, it is used for a defensive clearance when a player does not have sufficient time to control the ball or is unable to play it back to his goalkeeper. The over-head kick should not be used when close to other players, as it can create a dangerous play situation.

For an over-head kick, use the arms to help balance the weight of the body over the non-kicking leg, lean backward, and reach with the kicking leg to volley the ball back and over the head with the instep of the foot. (See Fig. 3–6.)

PIVOT KICK

On occasion a player is faced with a situation when he must suddenly turn on the ball to kick it in the right direction. This is known as the pivot or turn kick. To execute the pivot kick, run to the ball and time the approach so that the standing foot is turned, as it is placed next to the ball, to act as a pivot for the body when the kicking leg swings around and into the ball. If this kick is attempted off a sprint run, check the momentum of the body just before planting the standing foot next to the ball by leaning backward slightly. Use the arms to help maintain balance throughout the maneuver.

SCISSORS KICK

Although the scissors kick is not often seen in the game of soccer, it does occur and must be considered. The scissors kick is a quick method for reversing the direction of the ball or kicking straight away. To execute the scissors kick, jump up to meet the ball and with a scissor-like movement of the legs, use the instep of the left

Fig. 3–7. A scissors kick requires skill and care on the part of the kicker.

or right foot to kick the ball back over the head or straight away. Keep both hands down and ready to cushion the weight of the body when and if it hits the ground.

The scissors kick is discouraged by many instructors, as it often creates a dangerous play situation. Players must be cautioned not to use a scissors kick when close to other players. (See Fig. 3–7.)

Tips on Kicking

1. For an easy swing of the kicking foot, use an oblique approach to the ball.
2. For a low straight kick, plant the non-kicking foot alongside the ball, keep the head down, eyes on the ball, and the knee of the kicking foot over the ball.
3. For a long clearance kick, lean back and reach for the ball with the kicking foot.
4. Learn to kick equally well with both feet.
5. Learn to kick a moving ball.
6. Good kicks depend on proper timing. Timing comes with practice.
7. When executing a volley, use the arms to help maintain body balance.
8. Keep the ball low when kicking into the wind.
9. For a low volley kick, keep the toes down, get the body and knee over the ball, and meet it just before it strikes the ground.
10. For an accurate kick, focus the eyes on the ball and the shoe at the moment of impact.
11. Learn to kick from any angle.
12. When using a pivot kick, use the arms and lean backwards to maintain body balance.
13. A high kick often results when the non-kicking foot is placed too far behind the ball.
14. If the non-kicking foot is placed ahead of a stationary ball, the kicking foot will tend to drive the ball into the ground.
15. If the ball is rolling forward, place the non-kicking foot a little ahead of the ball and kick it at the proper time.
16. It is difficult to kick a ball accurately with the toe of the soccer shoe.

BALL CONTROL

Ball control is the key to the game of soccer because it affords and denies opportunities for players to score. In this respect, soccer is very similar to basketball. However, unlike basketball players, soccer players are not permitted to control the ball with their hands. Control the ball with parts of the body, other than the hands or arms, by mastering the following skills:

SOLE TRAP (ROLLING GROUND BALL)

Use a sole trap to control a rolling ball by reaching out and stopping the ball with either foot. Keep the toe of the trapping foot up and the heel down and maintain this position until contact

Fig. 3–8. Use a sole trap to control a rolling ball.

is made with the ball; then raise the heel and wedge the ball against the ground by applying pressure with the ball of the foot. (See Fig. 3–8.)

SOLE TRAP (BALL-OUT-OF-REACH)

Use a sole trap as a quick method for controlling a ball coming down out of reach, or for a bouncing ball. Reach out with the left or right foot to meet the ball as it bounces from the ground. Keep the trapping leg straight with the toes up and heel down. At the moment of contact, give slightly with the trapping leg by flexing the knee, and then push the ball down and wedge it against the ground. Move up on the ball immediately to gain complete control. (See Fig. 3–9.)

(1)　　　　　　　　　　　　　　　(2)

Fig. 3–9. Sole trap.
1. Reach for the ball with either foot.
2. Wedge the ball against the ground.

(1)   (2)

Fig. 3–10.   Trapping a high ball.
1. Judge the flight of the ball.
2. Wedge the ball against the ground.

SOLE TRAP (HIGH BALL)

To control a ball kicked high into the air, judge its flight and run to meet it. Just before contact, flex the knee and tilt the toes of the playing foot back. Trap the ball just as it strikes the ground. (See Fig. 3–10.)

OUTSIDE-OF-FOOT TRAP

Use the outside of the foot to trap a ball under the following conditions: to control a ground ball on the run, to screen an approaching ball from an opponent, or to control a ball approaching from the side. As the ball approaches, flex the knee and raise the trapping foot, turn it in slightly, and let it give with the ball at the moment of impact. Balance the weight of the body on the non-trapping leg. (See Fig. 3–11.)

INSIDE-OF-FOOT TRAP

To execute a trap with the inside of the foot, run to meet the ball and just before contact flex the knee and raise the trapping leg with the foot turned out slightly. At the moment of impact, let the foot give with the ball and balance the weight of the body on the non-trapping leg. (See Fig. 3–12.)

Fig. 3–11. Outside of foot trap.

1. Flex the knee and raise the trapping foot.
2. Turn the trapping foot in slightly.
3. Give with the trapping foot, at the moment of impact.
4. Balance the weight of the body over the non-trapping leg.

(1)

(1)   (2)   (3)   (4)

Fig. 3–12. Inside of foot trap.

1. Move toward the ball.
2. Raise the trapping leg with knee flexed and the foot turned out slightly.
3. Let the foot give with the ball.
4. Maintain close control.

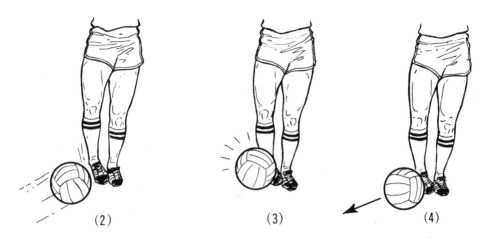

(2)   (3)   (4)

SHIN TRAP

The shin trap is an excellent method for teaching beginners the importance of running to meet the ball. To execute the shin trap, run to meet the ball and time it so that it hits the ground just in front of the feet as they are brought together. At the moment of impact, the legs relax and the knees drop over the ball. Move up on the ball to maintain complete control. (See Fig. 3–13.)

BALL CONTROL (WITH INSTEP OF FOOT)

Ball control with the instep of the foot is an advanced technique used to pull a ball to the ground or as a means of tapping it into the air for a follow-up kick. To trap the ball with the instep, raise the trapping leg, keep the arms away from the body, and balance the weight of the body over the opposite leg. At the moment of impact, cradle the ball in the instep and cushion it as the foot drops to the ground. To set up a follow-up kick, deaden the momentum of the ball by tapping it softly with the instep. (See Fig. 3–14.)

INSIDE-OF-FOOT TRAP (BOUNCING BALL)

Use the inside of the foot to gain control of a bouncing ball, or one that has been lofted into the air.

For an inside of the foot trap, flex the knee and lift the leg with the trapping foot slightly turned out. The weight of the body is balanced by the non-trapping leg and the distance of the ball from the player determines the position of the body. Cushion the ball

Fig. 3–13.   Shin trap.
1. Move toward the ball.
2. Time the approach of the ball.
3. The legs relax and the knees drop over the ball.
4. Stay close to the ball.

(1)

Fig. 3–14.   Use the instep of the foot to control the ball.

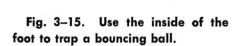

Fig. 3–15.   Use the inside of the foot to trap a bouncing ball.

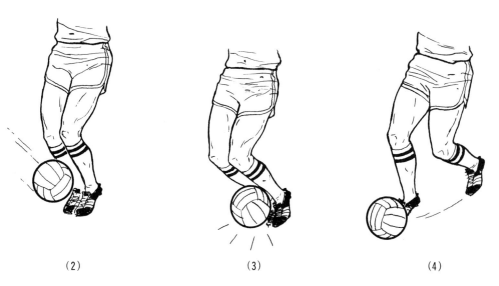

(2)   (3)   (4)

and drop it softly to the ground by giving with the foot at the moment of contact. (See Fig. 3–15.)

INSIDE-OF-LEG TRAP

Use the inside of the leg to pull the ball down quickly to the ground when it is approaching from the side and out of reach for a body or thigh trap. Reach for the ball with the trapping leg by leaning back and balancing the weight of the body over the opposite leg. Cushion the ball and drop it softly to the ground by giving with the leg at the moment of impact. (See Fig. 3–16.)

Fig. 3–16. When trapping with the inside of the leg, balance the weight of the body over the opposite leg.

Fig. 3–17. Inside of thigh trap.
1. Judge the flight of the ball and raise the trapping leg to meet it.
2. Cushion the ball with the inside of the thigh.
3. Drop the ball softly to the ground.
4. Maintain close control.

(1)

INSIDE-OF-THIGH TRAP

Use the inside of the thigh to control a ball approaching from the side. To execute the trap, raise the leg, bend the knee, and cushion the ball with the inside of the thigh. Drop the ball to the feet and maintain close control. (See Fig. 3–17.)

Occasionally, it is to a player's advantage to use the top of the thigh to control a bouncing ball. (See Fig. 3–18.)

WAIST TRAP

To drop a waist-high ball softly to the feet, move the shoulder over the ball, and give with the abdominal area of the body at the

Fig. 3–18. Top of thigh trap.

(2) (3) (4)

moment of impact. Keep both legs straight and the arms away from the body to help maintain balance and to avoid a hand or arm violation. (See Fig. 3–19.)

Fig. 3–19. Waist trap.

CHEST TRAP

For a chest trap, bend the knees, keep the upper part of the body slightly arched backwards, and give with the ball at the moment of impact. Keep the arms away from the body throughout the trap to help maintain balance and to avoid touching the ball with the hands or arms. To be an effective trap, the ball must drop softly from the chest to the feet. (See Fig. 3–20.)

(1)   (2)

Fig. 3–20.   Chest trap.

1. The chest gives with the ball.
2. Keep the arms away from the body.

HEAD TRAP

The head trap is a difficult skill to master but it is the mark of an expert performer. Although it is difficult and seldom used, occasionally it is the only possible method for bringing the ball under control.

To execute the head trap, cushion the ball against the forehead by bending the knees and giving with the head and neck at the moment of impact.   Drop the ball softly to the ground, as close to the feet as possible.   Follow up on the ball to maintain good control. (See Fig. 3–21.)

DRIBBLING

The dribble is the technique used by a player to move and maintain control of the ball, by propelling it with the feet. It is often used to avoid a would-be tackler, to set up a passing or shooting situation, or to take advantage of an opening that calls for individual effort. In short, the strategy of the dribble is to maintain possession of the ball until a pass to a teammate or a shot at goal is in order.

The mechanics of the dribble involve pushing the ball with the inside or outside of the foot while walking, jogging, or running.   In

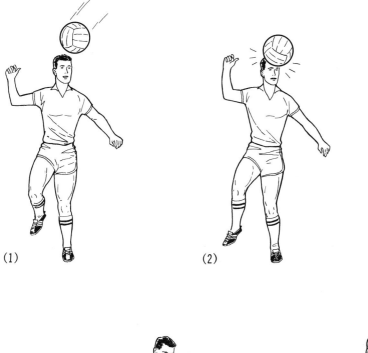

(1)   (2)

(3)   (4)

Fig. 3–21.   Head trap.

1. Judge the flight of the ball.
2. Cushion the ball against the forehead.
3. Drop the ball close to the feet.
4. Stay close to the ball.

Fig. 3–22. Use the dribble to move and maintain control of the ball.

Fig. 3–23. Keep the body between the ball and the opponent.

addition, good dribbling requires faking, screening, and change of pace tactics. For maximum ball control, dribble with the inside of the foot and keep the body close to the ball. (See Fig. 3–22.) For a fast dribble, use alternate taps with the insides of the feet. In close quarters play the ball so that the body screens it from an opponent. (See Fig. 3–23.)

FEINTING

A feint is a pretense of moving in one direction while actually moving in another. Its purpose is to out-maneuver an opponent by drawing him into a false move. Any false move which successfully out-maneuvers an opponent constitutes feinting. A body swerve is a common feint, as are with feints with the feet, legs, or other parts of the body. Feints are numerous and varied, and their effectiveness is largely dependent upon individual reaction patterns.

Good feinting comes with practice and experience; a player must train his reflexes for successful patterns.

The feint is an important facet in the art of dribbling. In the parlance of the sport, it is known as "selling the dummy." To feint off the dribble, swerve with the body in one direction and then suddenly change direction, or tap the ball in one direction and suddenly reverse it in the opposite direction.

Feinting is not confined to the man with the ball. A feint by a player trying to get possession of the ball is an excellent method for countering a move by a dribbler. Use the feint to force a dribbler into a mistake. Feinting tactics are also used to counter man-to-man marking, or as preliminary moves before moving into an open space to receive a pass.

PASSING

Passing is one of the most artistic features of the game; it calls for skillful and systematic distribution of the ball from player to player. It is also one of soccer's unique skills because its success hinges upon the co-operation of at least two players. The theory of passing is that the player who has the ball should, when in danger of losing it or when it enables his team to make progress towards the opponents' goal, send it on to one of his teammates who is for the time unmarked. The receiver must position himself to receive the ball, and the passer must send the ball to him accurately and in the most effective manner. Consequently, when teaching the passing phase of the game, it is important to emphasis the roles that must be played by both the passer and the receiver. One is dependent upon the other and without teamwork the passing game becomes ineffective.

Use the following passes to get the ball to a teammate.

PUSH PASS

The push pass is an accurate method for moving the ball on the ground by kicking it with the inside of the foot. Although it is usually associated with the short-passing game, it can be effectively used up to distances of 35 to 40 yards.

To execute the push pass, get the body over the ball, raise the kicking foot slightly, turn it out, and contact the ball between the heel and the big toe. At the moment of impact, balance the weight of the body over the opposite foot. Keep the head down, eyes on ball, and follow through for a short distance. The power for the pass is generated by the swinging movement of the leg.

PASS WITH OUTSIDE OF FOOT

A pass with the outside of the foot is a quick and deceptive method for moving the ball to a teammate. As a rule, the effective distance of this pass is limited to short-passing situations.

To execute the pass, raise and rotate the kicking leg inward, and with the weight of the body balanced over the non-kicking leg, straighten the knee and jab at the ball with the outside of the instep and follow through. (See Fig. 3–24.)

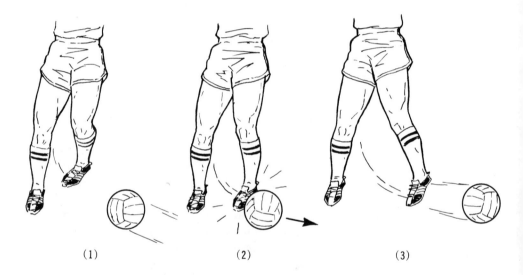

(1)   (2)   (3)

Fig. 3–24.   Pass with the outside of the foot.
1. Raise and rotate the kicking leg inward.
2. Straighten the knee and jab at the ball with the outside of the instep.
3. Follow through.

HEEL PASS

A pass with the heel is a deceptive method for touching the ball back to a teammate. As a rule the player to whom the ball is passed calls the play. Although the heel pass is not often used, it can be very effective in tight situations, especially around the penalty area.

For a pass with the heel, place the non-kicking foot alongside the ball, step over the ball with the kicking foot, flex the knee, and kick the ball backward with the heel. (See Fig. 3–25.)

Fig. 3–25. Pass with the heel.

Fig. 3–26. The sole pass.

SOLE PASS

The strategy for the sole and heel passes is basically the same; however, the mechanics for executing the two skills are slightly different. For a sole pass place the non-passing foot alongside the ball, step the on ball with the sole of the other foot, flex the knee, and roll the ball back to a teammate. (See Fig. 3–26.)

HEADING

Heading is a method for propelling the ball. It is a skill unique to the game of soccer and a player's skills are not complete without it Heading has many functions, namely: ball control (see head trap—Fig. 3–21), defensive clearances, passing, and scoring.

DEFENSIVE CLEARANCE

The height of the ball and the challenge from the opposition determine whether or not a player jumps to meet the ball or heads it from a stationary position. When jumping to meet the ball, take a short run, whenever possible, and use a single-foot takeoff. Gen-

erate power for the head play by swaying the upper part of the body
back and then swinging it forward to meet the ball with the upper
part of the forehead. Stiffen the neck muscles at the moment of
impact. Keep the eyes on the ball throughout the maneuver, including the follow through. (See Fig. 3–27.)

HEAD PASS

The ideal head pass is directed to a teammate's feet. For a head
pass to a teammate, tilt the head downward and hit the ball with
the forehead, just below the hairline. When heading from a stationary stance, keep one foot ahead of the other and rock back on
the ball of the rear foot to get added power for the forward swing
with the upper part of the body. (See Fig. 3–28.) When jumping
to meet the ball, turn the body at the waist and head the ball in the
desired direction.

Fig. 3–27. Defensive heading.

Fig. 3–28. An ideal head pass is
one directed to a teammate's feet.

For directional heading, turn at the waist.

HEAD SHOT

For a head shot at goal, jump, dive, or drive for the ball, and head it downward into the corner of the goal, away from the goal-keeper. (See Fig. 3–29.)

Fig. 3–29. Heading allows for a quick shot at goal.

TACKLING AND INTERCEPTION

Tackling and interception are the methods used to regain possession of the ball when it has been lost to the opposition. To tackle means to take the ball away from an opponent, or force him to get rid of it at a disadvantage. Interception depends upon a player's ability to take advantage of poor technique on the part of the opposition, along with a sense of timing and feeling for the game. Anticipating the opponents' moves is a vital factor in intercepting the ball or cutting off a play. The ability to intercept the ball requires a keen knowledge of the game's strategy and usually comes with experience.

When a player has clear possession of the ball, his opponents have one of two alternatives: to take the ball away with a tackle, or to force the player with the ball to make a mistake. Around the penalty area, tackle the man with the ball, or use the sole or inside of the foot to smother an attempted shot.

The rules permit players to use a shoulder-to-shoulder charge when contesting for possession of the ball, providing the shoulder charge is made when both players are within playing distance of the ball.

ONE-FOOT TACKLE

The one-foot tackle can be used when approaching a player head-on, from the side, or from the rear. Watch the movement of the ball and once a decision to tackle is made, move in forcefully with one foot and balance the weight of the body over the other leg.

Fig. 3–30.   One-foot tackle.

1. Watch the ball—not the man.
2. Block the ball against the opponent's foot.
3. Roll the ball over the dribbler's foot.

(1)

Sliding tackle. (Photo by Michael Jencks)

Block the ball against the opponent's foot and attempt to gain possession of the ball with the tackling foot by rolling it over the dribbler's foot. To maintain a sustained effort, keep the weight of the body over the non-tackling leg. (See Fig. 3–30.)

SLIDING TACKLE

The sliding tackle is a difficult skill to perform. If it is not properly executed, it can result in a dangerous play situation. Although the sliding tackle is permitted by the international rules, at some

(2)

(3)

Fig. 3–31. Throw-in.

1. The hands are on opposite sides of the ball.
2. Draw the ball over and well behind the head.
3. Bend the knees forward and the trunk backwards.
4. Throw the ball forward and directly over the head.
5. Follow through with a simultaneous extension of both arms.

levels of competition the rule has been modified and the sliding tackle is not permitted.

Use the sliding tackle as a means of hooking the ball away from a player when it is the only method of reaching the ball. Slide into the tackle by falling on to one side. Contact the ground with the side of the leg, thigh, or buttock, bend the knee closest to the ground and reach out with the other leg to hook the ball with the instep of the foot. At the same time, balance the weight of the trunk of the body by placing the near hand on the ground with the elbow bent. Once the tackle is completed, recover to a standing position as soon as possible.

THROW-IN

The ball is ruled out of play when it has completely crossed the touch line, either on the ground or in the air. The ball is put back into play at the point on the touch line where it went out of play with a two-hand throw in any direction by a player of the team opposite to that of the player who last touched it. Both feet must maintain contact with the ground and be placed on or outside the touch line at the moment the ball is thrown. However, a player is permitted to come up to his toes, or drag one foot on the ground. The mechanics for the throw-in are covered by the rules of the game and must be followed accordingly. When the ball is improperly thrown in, the throw-in is awarded to the opposing team.

The throw-in is, in effect, a two-hand pass to a teammate. To execute the throw-in, place both hands, fingers spread, on opposite sides of the ball, draw the ball over and well behind the head and, at the same time, bend the knees forward and the trunk backwards. Throw the ball forward and directly over the head with a strong swing and simultaneous extension of both arms. As the hands pass over the head, straighten the knees and thrust the trunk forward and over the hips. Flick the hands and fingers as the ball is released and follow through with both arms in a smooth, co-ordinated manner. Keep both feet together or place one foot behind the other. For added power and distance, or if it serves a tactical advantage, take a few run-up steps to the above-mentioned positions. The rules permit a run-up to the point where the ball is declared out-of-bounds. (See Fig. 3–31.)

GOAL TENDING

The goalkeeper's chief duty is to prevent the ball from passing through the goal. His position is very demanding: it requires a combination of speed, agility, and timing plus the ability to handle the ball with the hands as well as the feet in a flawless manner. In addition, the goalkeeper must blend with all of his goal-tending skills a sense of anticipation which calls for the right move at the right time. Use the following skills for goal tending.

Goalkeeping requires speed, agility, and all-around skill.

 (1)    (2)    (3)

Fig. 3–32.   Fielding.

1. Drop the knee to the ground.
2. Place the palms of the hands under the ball.
3. Stand up and keep the ball close to the body.

FIELDING

To field a low ball, face the direction from which the ball is coming, with the lines of the shoulders and hips at right angles to the line of flight of the ball. Drop the left or right knee to the ground, place the palms of the hands under the ball, and pull it snugly into the body. (See Fig. 3–32.)

CATCHING

To handle a shot that is off the ground, face the kicker so that some part of the body is behind the hands and arms when the ball is caught. Whenever possible, catch the ball against the body. Keep the elbows into the body, palms of hands up, and get a firm hold on the ball.

Whenever possible, catch the ball against the body. (Photo by Michael Jencks)

For an over-head catch, reach with both hands behind the ball, fingers spread. Cushion the force of the shot by giving slightly with the hands, at the moment of impact. Bring the ball down immediately and hug it against the chest. (See Fig. 3–33.)

Fig. 3–33. Over-head catch.
1. Reach with both hands, fingers spread.
2. Give with the hands to cushion the force of the shot.
3. Hug the ball against the chest.

DIVING

Diving is a technique used to get possession of the ball when a shot does not allow for enough time to get the body behind the ball or when the ball is just out of reach. Timing and anticipation play important roles in determining how quickly a goalkeeper can react to a diving situation. It is essential to maintain a stance that will afford the balance needed to move in any direction. Keep the arms in front of the body in a ready position, with the palms of the hands facing the kicker. The weight of the body is balanced over both legs and ready to push off on the ball of either foot. Once the dive is made, the technique for handling the ball is similar to that used for the over-head catch. (See Fig. 3–34.)

To handle a low ball at close quarters, roll into the ball, and pull it quickly into the body. (See Fig. 3–35.)

Fig. 3–34.   A goalkeeper must learn when to react to a diving situation.

Fig. 3–35.   Roll into the ball with the head down and away from the opponent.

In some situations the goalkeeper's only alternative is to tip the ball over the cross-bar. (Photo by Michael Jencks)

DEFLECTING

In a tight situation, it is often advisable for the goalkeeper to tip the ball over the cross-bar or around the goal post. To deflect a high shot at goal, use one or both hands to tip the ball up and over the cross-bar.

FISTING

Fisting is a quick method for clearing the ball when the goalkeeper does not have time to catch the ball, or when it cannot be

In a tight situation, a goalkeeper must be prepared to clear the ball by fisting it with one or both fists.

reached with both hands. In a tight situation, jump to meet the ball and use one or both fists to clear it from the mouth of the goal.

THROWING

A throw is an excellent method for clearing the ball to a teammate. The most effective throw is one to the feet of a teammate who has good field position and is unmarked. For a long toss, use an overhand or sling throw. For a short pass use an underhand throw or roll it on the ground. (See Fig. 3–36.)

KICKING

Kicking plays an important role in goal tending. If there is insufficient time for the goalkeeper to handle the ball, he must resort to a quick kick. Quite often the goalkeeper, rather than a back,

Fig. 3–36. Throws by goalkeeper.

1. Overhand throw.
2. Sling throw.
3. Underhand throw.

Fig. 3–37. Drop-kick.

1. Drop the ball to the ground.
2. Kick it with the instep of the foot just as it bounces from the ground.

kicks the ball back into play during a goal-kick situation. The punt volley and drop kick are excellent methods for a goalie to clear the ball to a teammate.

For a goal kick, use a long kick with the instep of the foot, or a short push pass to a teammate who is unmarked. To execute a long clearance pass to a teammate, use a punt volley or a drop kick. The drop kick is a quick method for sending a long, low kick to a teammate. It requires perfect timing. Drop the ball to the ground and kick it with the instep of the foot just as it bounces from the ground. To add power and distance to the drop kick or punt volley move into the kick by taking one or two forward strides. (See Fig. 3–37.)

GOALKEEPER'S HAND DRIBBLE

The rules permit the goalkeeper to handle and carry the ball anywhere in the penalty area, providing not more than four steps are taken without bouncing the ball on the ground.[1] Carrying and bouncing the ball in the penalty area plays an important role in the strategy of the game. The goalkeeper must determine when it is advantageous to work the ball out to the edge of the penalty area with a series of steps and bounces before clearing to a teammate.

Goalkeepers should develop techniques for carrying the ball in the penalty area that will avoid interception by the opposition. This involves the ability to combine the bounce with faking, dodging, and the use of teammates for screening tactics.

[1] For recent interpretations of the international rules for the goalkeeper's hand dribble and the punishment for any infringement thereof, the reader is referred to the rules of the United States Soccer Football Association. For interpretations of the rule in intercollegiate, or interscholastic soccer, use The National Intercollegiate Athletic Association's Annual Soccer Guide.

4

Training and Coaching

Training in soccer is primarily concerned with helping players improve their performance in the game. It should consider all aspects of the game, namely: attitude, skill, stamina, strategy, strength, teamwork, and timing. Through a series of planned activities, a training program must afford opportunities for players to develop a level of physical fitness and skill proficiency, along with a degree of mental alertness, that will contribute to optimum game performances.

Training methods vary in all sports and soccer is no exception. Techniques of training are constantly changing and improving. When designing a training program for soccer, consider the individual players involved; the level of competition at which they perform; the time allocated to training; and the length of the soccer season.

For age-group soccer (ages six to twelve), the game should be a fun-type activity. It is important to expose youngsters to soccer during their formative years; however, age-group players should not be subjected to intensive training routines. Instead, the emphasis should be on skill training and informal soccer matches.

At higher levels of competition—high school, college, club, and professional soccer—players must be in top physical condition. The individual who participates in highly competitive soccer must maintain good health and adhere to strict training rules. Good healthful meals, plenty of sleep, no smoking or drinking, and a great deal of game-related exercise are important elements in every player's routine. To appreciate the need for a training routine that will insure ideal condition, there is a need for a general understanding of muscular fatigue.

Muscular fatigue is the loss of the muscles' normal function because of the accumulation of waste products when the muscles are subjected to prolonged or intense work. The cause of the accumulation may lie in the body's failure to remove the waste products from the muscles or in its failure to supply the oxygen necessary for the oxidation of the lactic acid, because of the incapacity of either the circulatory or the respiratory system to meet the muscles' increased demands. Therefore, a player's endurance is governed, to a large degree, by the rapidity with which the waste products can be removed from the muscles.

Physical training develops endurance by increasing the efficiency of the heart and circulatory system. The heart is a muscle and, like any other muscle, it tends to increase in efficiency and size with exercise. An athlete's heart beat is slower and stronger than that of a non-athlete. It has the ability to pump through the blood stream the necessary oxygen and fuel to the muscles.

Training also increases the capacity of the lungs, which in turn supply the blood with larger amounts of oxygen to rid the blood stream of waste products. Efficient lungs, together with a strong heart, increase the ability of the muscles to function in such a way that they can contract over and over without undue fatigue. This is the type of endurance that is needed for soccer.

In starting to train for soccer, always allow for plenty of time. Plan the whole training process so that a steady progress can be made toward attaining a peak condition that will withstand any work of equal intensity that might be experienced in a game. Generally, a six-week training period allows sufficient time for players to improve their condition to the standard needed for match play.

The type of fitness needed for soccer must be related to the requirements of the game. Sports movements differ, and it is generally agreed by most authorities that fitness in one sport does not necessarily carry over into another sport. Most sports have unique movements and require a type of training that is specifically related to the activity. Soccer is a game that calls for unique movements with or without control of the ball. During the course of a game, players use a full range and an infinite variety of movements. Change of pace tactics include: walking, jogging, running, sprinting, and jumping. Many of the movements involve sudden stops and changes of direction. To help maintain balance, players must keep the body's center of gravity closer to the ground. When moving with or near the ball, movements should be made with the arms held in a horizontal position to help maintain balance and to minimize the chance of handling the ball.

To cope with the physical demands of the game, players must develop their physical fitness, increase their strength, and improve their skills. Physical fitness combined with skill provides a margin of safety that can not be achieved in any other way. Physical fitness improves a soccer player's ability to move and it improves his endurance. Strength enables a player to cope with the stresses and strains that result from the requirements of the game, and it is also a factor in a player's performance; while skill enables a player to apply the basic fundamentals to the movement patterns of the game in the most proficient manner. All of these factors are interrelated and must be integrated into the training program.

To be physically fit for soccer, a player needs agility, balance, endurance, flexibility, power, and strength. Many of these qualities can be best achieved through drills that also contribute to skill training. Whenever possible, training for soccer should simulate actual play conditions. Static drills that limit players to a choice of one skill are meaningless. Drills become meaningful when they are recognized by the players as an integral part of actual playing technique. For best results, use drills that provide a series of options from which, depending upon the situation, a player must make an intelligent choice.

The drills described in this chapter do not represent an exhaustive list of training techniques. They are suggested as examples of training methods designed to serve a twofold purpose: first, to perfect the basic fundamentals described in Chapter 3; and second, to prepare players physically and mentally for match play. Coaches and players are encouraged to use other drills and, whenever possible, to create additional training techniques that will contribute to these objectives.

PROGRAMMING THE TRAINING SESSION

In many soccer programs time is limited, and it must be used to best advantage. An organizational plan that budgets the time allocated to a training program tends to insure quality work for all the players. To facilitate the training process, program daily training sessions by assigning drills to various teaching and training stations designated on and around the field of play. (See Fig. 4–1.) Note that the majority of the stations are organized on the field of play, as it is the one facility which is common to a soccer program. The kick board and the captive ball assembly are recommended as valuable adjuncts to a training program. Skill training for a large group is also enhanced by a program that uses a large number of practice balls. For some drills, notably dribbling, almost any kind of ball is acceptable. Old soccer balls should never be discarded.

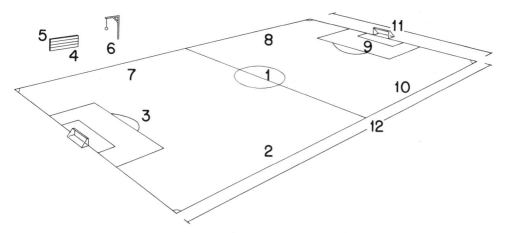

Fig. 4–1. Teaching and training stations.

Keep a large supply of practice balls on the practice field to give more players more opportunities to train with the ball.

The players should not be expected to cover the entire circuit of stations on any given day. Actually, players should concentrate most of their training at the stations that offer drills that relate specifically to the duties and responsibilities of their respective positions. For example, training for goalkeepers should stress goal tending skills and related drills. However, from time to time, players other then goalkeepers should devote a portion of their training routine to all aspects of the game. This is important for a system of play that anticipates total team involvement, both on offense and defense.

The following teaching and training stations, along with the assigned drills and training techniques, are offered as an organizational plan for training soccer players:

STATION ONE

1. Warm-up Exercises
2. Circle Dribbling Drill
3. Close Quarter Dribbling Drill
4. Dribble and Pass Drill

Use the center circle for conducting *warm-up exercises* and as the station for orienting the entire squad to the schedule for the day. The boundary line of the center circle can easily accommodate twenty-two players for warm-up drills and certain skill training techniques. When more space is needed have some of the players form a larger concentric circle. The following exercises are typical of the types that can be used for warming up:

1. Walking and Skipping
2. Jogging
3. Jumping To Head an Imaginary Ball
4. Duck and Bear Walks
5. Burpee's Exercise
6. Jogging with Knees High
7. Deep Knee Bends
8. Side Straddle Hops
9. Running Backwards
10. Short Sprints

The warm-up phase of the training session is the logical time to introduce the players to interval-type training. From the center of the circle, the coach can determine the appropriate activities, their pace, and the length of the work and rest intervals. The interval period of time between exercises is usually devoted to walking, jogging, or exercising at a slower pace.

Interval training applies the physiological over-load principle by increasing the pace and number of repetitions, by decreasing the interval, or by doing both. Eventually, when an interval training program is intensified, the work load for each individual may best be determined by his heart rate recovery. A fast recovery to a near normal pulse rate during the resting interval is the best index of excellent physical condition.

The *circle dribbling drill* combines skill and fitness training. With each player in possession of a ball, the drill involves walking, jogging, and sprinting while executing a dribble along the boundary line of the center circle. For variations of the drill, use sudden stop and go commands, as well as a command that reverses the direction of the dribblers. This is a very demanding drill and lends itself to interval-type training. (See Fig. 4–2.)

For the *close-quarter dribbling drill,* each player of a group, which varies in size from five to twenty players, dribbles a ball within the boundaries of the center circle. By dribbling in any direction within the confines of the center circle, the players develop the ability to maneuver with the ball in tight spaces. At the same time, each player develops an awareness of the other players who are moving in all directions. Generally, three to four minutes of close-quarter dribbling, executed at a moderate to fast pace, challenges the physical fitness of most soccer players. (See Fig. 4–3.)

Fig. 4–2.   Circle dribbling drill.

Fig. 4–3.   Close-quarter dribbling.

The *dribble-pass drill* offers skill training in dribbling, passing, and trapping. In addition, it stresses teamwork and emphasizes the need for players to use their peripheral vision when dribbling with the ball. During the drill players should be encouraged to keep the ball on the ground and to use the inside and outside of the foot for both passing and trapping.

To organize the dribble-pass drill, assign one player to the flank of a teammate who is standing on the boundary line of the center circle. The distance between the two players should be from 10 to 15 yards. The paired players should move in the same direction, with or without the ball, and attempt to maintain their relative positions. The tempo of the drill may be controlled by the coach with commands for passing, reversing direction, sprinting, stopping, etc.

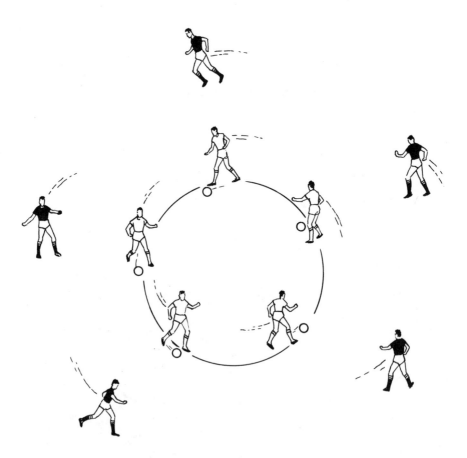

Fig. 4–4. Dribble-pass drill.

To develop teamwork, the player without the ball should be given the responsibility of calling to his teammate for a pass. When passing the ball, the passer should lead his teammate with the ball. (See Fig. 4–4.)

STATION TWO (DRIBBLING AND TACKLING)

1. Beat Three Drill
2. Two-on-One Drill
3. Pressure Tackling Drill

The *beat three drill* gives players opportunities to practice dribbling and tackling, as a player attempts to dribble past three defenders who are positioned in a vertical line about 15 yards apart. To avoid excessive lateral movement by the dribbler, the station for the drill is restricted by markers [1] to a width of 20 yards. The defenders are restricted to a vertical zone of approximately 5 yards behind their assigned positions. If the dribbler gets past the first defender, he challenges the second defender, and then the third. When the dribbler loses possession of the ball, due to the action of any one of the three defenders, he assumes the position of the last defender, and the other defenders move up in their positions, with the number one defender moving out to the end of the line to take a turn as a dribbler. A tackle is considered successful when the defender either gains possession of the ball or kicks the ball away from the dribbler, providing it happens within the boundaries of his station. The drill is designed to keep seven to nine players quite active. (See Fig. 4–5.)

For a variation of this drill, create a *two-on-one situation* by having two players use dribbling and short-passing tactics in an attempt to out-maneuver each of the three defenders. The defenders for the two-on-one situation are restricted to the designated zones of the beat three drill. If the two attackers fail to successfully out-maneuver any one of the three defenders, they assume the roles of defenders by replacing the tacklers at the second and third defensive positions. At the same time the first and second defenders rotate to form a team at the end of the attacking line and the third defender moves up to cover the first defensive position. If the two-man attacking team is successful against all three defenders, they go back to the end of the attacking line for another turn on offense. (See Fig. 4–6.)

---

[1] The rubber cone-shaped markers used for street and highway construction are ideal for marking the zones of the various stations.

Fig. 4–5.   Beat three drill.

For a *pressure tackling drill,* six or more dribblers take turns challenging a lone defender. To keep the pressure on the tackler, each attacker should be in possession of a ball and ready to challenge the defender just as soon as the defender completes his effort against the preceding dribbler. The pressure tackling drill is highly recommended for interval-type training. (See Fig. 4–7.)

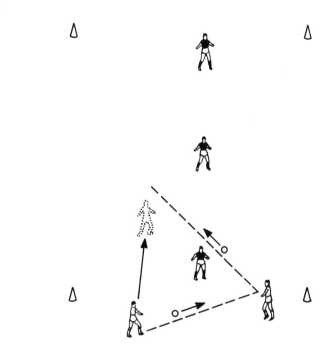

Fig. 4–6. Two-on-one drill.

STATION THREE

1. Passing and Shooting Drill
2. Pressure Training Drill
3. Deep Optional Drill

The drills for one of the goal stations are designed primarily to help players improve their shooting ability and to practice scoring situations that tend to repeat themselves in and around the penalty area. The drills also afford training for a goalkeeper who attempts to save the shots taken at the goal. The drills recommended for station three can also make a valuable contribution to physical

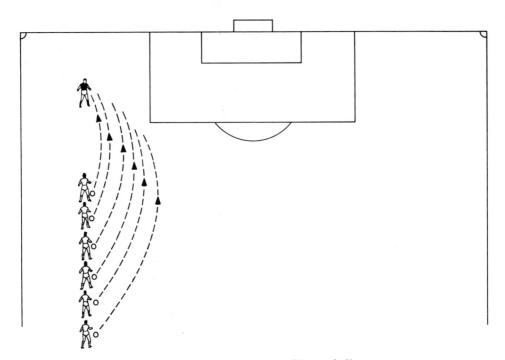

Fig. 4–7.   Pressure tackling drill.

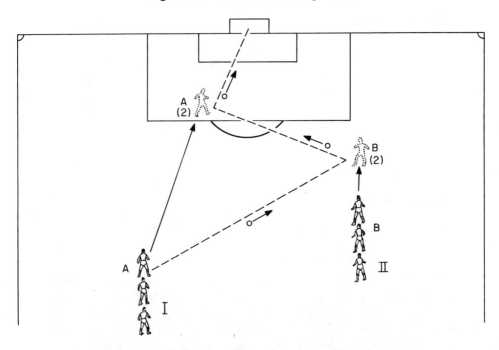

Fig. 4–8.   Passing and shooting drill.

fitness training, depending upon the tempo at which they are conducted.

To conduct the *passing and shooting drill*, assign Group I to one side of the field, in a zone that is approximately 30 yards from the penalty area, and Group II to the opposite side of the field, in a zone approximately 20 yards from the penalty area. Player A from Group I starts the drill by passing to player B who runs from Group II to meet the ball. Player B returns the ball to player A by directing a pass to a zone just inside the penalty area. Player A should run to meet the ball and, whenever possible, attempt a first-time shot at goal. The drill should give players opportunities to kick the ball with either foot, and they should have the option of controlling the ball before passing or shooting. (See Fig. 4–8.)

Pressure training for both a shooter and a goalkeeper results when a series of balls are served to a player who is positioned just inside of the penalty area. The shooter should be facing the server so that he will have to turn with the ball as he kicks it toward the goal. To keep pressure on the shooter, two or three servers should take turns serving a new ball to the kicker just as soon as he completes his shot. For additional pressure, assign a defender to play between the shooter and the goal. To improve the kicking skill of both feet, the serves should be directed to either side of the kicker. The goalkeeper is under pressure, as he attempts to save each of the shots taken by the kicker. For best results the drill requires a supply of eight to ten soccer balls.

The *deep optional drill* recreates a situation that is common to the game of soccer; a situation during which a wingman is in possession of the ball and near the opponents' goal line. As a rule the shooting angle for a wingman is poor; consequently, he is usually faced with a series of options that involve crossing the ball to a teammate who is in a better position to score. The cross options include: a hard driving pass, about waist high, across the mouth of the goal; a pass back to a teammate who moves forward for a shot at goal; or a chip shot to a teammate who is near the far side of the goal area. (See Fig. 4–9.) Note that a defending fullback is covering a possible breakthrough by the wingman and that the wingman's teammates are anticipating one of the cross options as they maneuver for position. The wingman's choice of options is determined by how the defenders react to the attacking players' movements.

Initially, the option drill should be conducted without defenders; however, as soon as the attacking players learn their assignments, defenders should be added to the drill.

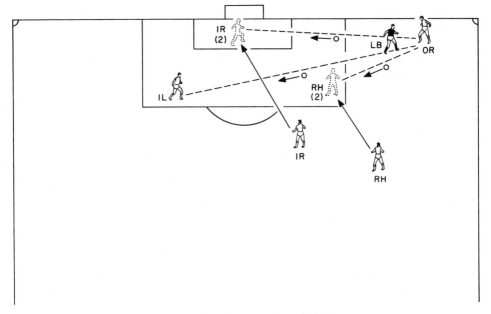

Fig. 4–9. Deep optional drill.

STATION FOUR (FIRST-TIME KICKING DRILL)

To simulate defensive first-time kicking under competitive conditions, use one side of the bounding board as a station for conducting a *first-time kicking drill.* To execute the drill, players take turns kicking the ball after it rebounds off the board. A player is allowed only one kick during his turn, and he is automatically eliminated under the following conditions: if he fails to use a first-time kick; if the ball fails to hit the board after it is kicked; if the ball is permitted to come to a dead stop before it is played; or if he kicks out of turn. The drill continues until all but one of the players are eliminated. In addition to learning to kick accurately under the pressure of time and competition, this drill provides players with continuous opportunities for pivot kicking. It is an excellent drill for all the players, especially those who are primarily concerned with defense.

STATION FIVE (GOAL-TENDING DRILLS)

The other side of the bounding board is an excellent station for conducting a training routine for a goalkeeper. The routine should include opportunities for a goalkeeper to learn the goal-tending skills described in Chapter 3 and, at the same time, improve his physical fitness.

For skill training, the coach, or a player, should serve the ball to the goalkeeper in a manner that will force him to use one of the basic goal-tending skills. Initially the ball should be thrown in a deliberate manner to an area of the bounding board. Gradually, the tempo of the throw should be increased. Eventually, the server should attempt to kick the ball past the goalkeeper. To save the ball before it hits the bounding board, the goalkeeper must choose the most appropriate technique from his repertory of defensive skills. Proper placements by the player serving the ball can simulate game conditions for the goalkeeper. It gives the goalie opportunities to practice the majority of the basic goal-saving techniques. This is a form of specialized training that is not always derived from a scrimmage or a game.

For physical fitness training, goalkeepers should be required to participate in many of the training routines prescribed for other players. In addition, a specialized routine that emphasizes pressure training is recommended. The following is an example of a basic pressure training routine for a goalkeeper:

1. A server alternates throwing two soccer balls toward the goalkeeper who catches and returns each throw to the server.

2. A server alternates rolling two soccer balls toward the goalkeeper who catches and returns each roll to the server.

3. With the goalkeeper positioned on his knees in front of the bounding board, a server alternates rolling a soccer ball to either side of the goalkeeper. The goalkeeper should reach or dive for the ball and return it to the server. This drill also teaches the goalkeeper to fall on his side when he dives for the ball.

4. Use the same procedure as drill number three with the exception of the throw, which should be high enough off the ground to force the goalkeeper into a diving save.

5. From a standing position, a goalkeeper defends the bounding board as a kicker shoots from a distance of 12 to 20 yards.

6. Two players take turns throwing a ball toward the board and at a height which forces the goalkeeper to use tipping or fisting techniques in order to clear the ball.

7. A player kicks the ball against the bounding board from a position behind the goalkeeper, who is approximately 5 yards from the board and facing it. The purpose of this drill is for the goalkeeper to react to the rebounding action of the ball by attempting to catch it as soon as possible. This drill is an excellent method of improving the reactions of goalkeepers to unexpected game situations. To make it difficult for the goalkeeper, the kicker should vary the angle of his shots.

8. Line up ten soccer balls at a distance of 15 yards from the bounding board and have two players take turns attempting to kick the ball past the goalkeeper. The next shot should be taken just as soon as the goalkeeper has had time to recover to a defensive position.

For best results these drills should stress interval training. If more work is needed, a drill should be repeated after a short resting interval.

STATION SIX (HEADING DRILLS)

The captive ball assembly and the area adjacent to it are recommended as a station for conducting specific heading drills. In addition, heading technique should be stressed when it becomes a tactical option in other drills or in game situations. To be prepared for tactical opportunities for heading, players must master the heading techniques described in Chapter 3.

When teaching heading to beginners or to age-group players, the ball should be partially inflated, as a beginner is more apt to head a softer ball with confidence. As soon as players have had sufficient time to learn heading technique, the ball should be inflated to the pressure recommended for their level of play.

For a *continuous straight-away heading drill* with a captive ball, adjust the level of the ball at a height to which a player can jump with relative ease. The player should repeat the heading technique by timing his next jump to the return swing of the ball.

The area adjacent to the captive ball assembly is recommended for drills involving groups of players. For a *heading drill with movement,* use two lines of players and a server. The server throws the ball toward a player in line A who, in turn, heads it to a player from line B, who calls for the ball as he moves into an open space. After the players complete the drill, they go to the ends of the

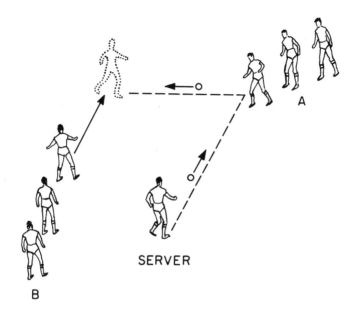

Fig. 4–10. Heading drill with movement.

opposite lines. Eventually, defenders should be assigned to the receivers. (See Fig. 4–10.)

To teach heading technique to players who are primarily concerned with defense, use a drill in which a defender must contest his jump for the ball with an opponent who is positioned in front of him. A server should toss the ball to a height just above their heads. Initially, the attacker should offer token resistance to the defender; however, as soon as the defender develops his skill, the resistance of the attacker should become more active.

STATION SEVEN (TWO-ON-ONE DRILL)

Station seven, situated along the touch line, serves as an area for staging a *two-on-one drill*, which emphasizes the throw-in, along with ball control, tackling, passing, and heading. To organize the drill, assign players to Groups A, B, and C. (See Fig. 4–11.) The drill begins with the first player in Group A throwing in to the first player from Group B who, in turn, controls the ball and passes it back to the thrower, who moves onto the field of play as soon as

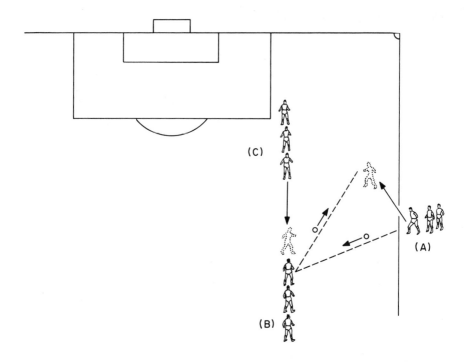

Fig. 4–11. The two-on-one drill emphasizes the throw-in, along with ball control, tackling, passing, and heading.

the ball is played by his teammate. The first player from Group C plays the role of a defender, as he attempts to take the ball away from the receiver. The distance of the player in Group C from the player receiving the throw will determine, for the most part, the amount of time the receiver will have for controlling and passing the ball. At the completion of each turn, the players should rotate to the end of the line of the next group.

When working with beginners, the defenders should be positioned at a distance that will give the receivers ample time to control and pass the ball. Gradually, the distance between the two players should be decreased until they are positioned as they would be in an actual game situation. In a tight throw-in situation, the receiver will quite often head the ball back to his teammate.

STATION EIGHT (PLAY-BACK DRILL)

The half of the field adjacent to the touch line provides the space needed to conduct the *play-back drill*. The drill involves three players in a sequence pattern that includes a pass, a return pass, and progress downfield. The object of the drill is for one player to kick the ball into the air and toward two other players who are positioned 20 to 25 yards away and ready to compete for the ball in order to play it back to the server. The play-back drill lends itself to pressure training, along with skill development in kicking, trapping, heading, and tackling. In addition, it helps foster teamwork.

Ideally, the drill should result in the receiver quickly heading the ball back to the kicker. Whenever a head play is not possible, the receiver must use other ball control and kicking skills that are appropriate to the situation. If the server fails to get the ball into the air, or if he kicks it past the two receivers, play should stop and the drill be restarted. To create an opportunity for a heading situation, the kicker should use a chip or lob pass and direct it toward a space that is close to both players. On occasion, the kicker's pass should favor one or the other receiver. If the receivers do not know to whom the ball is to be served, they will stay fairly close together.

In Fig. 4–12 player A directs his kick to player B who must contend with opposition from player C for the play back to the server. The drill repeats itself as soon as the ball is played back to the

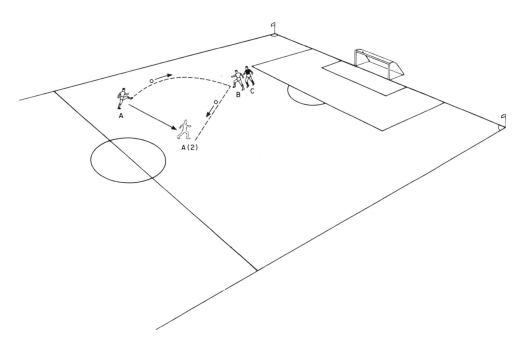

Fig. 4–12. Play-back drill.

server, and players progressively move downfield toward the goal line. When the receivers reach the goal line, the direction of the drill is reversed. From time to time, the players should rotate their assignments for the drill.

STATION NINE

1. Corner Kick Drill
2. Penalty Kick Drill

For a *corner kick drill,* assign players to sub-stations A, B, and C. (See Fig. 4–13.) A player from Group A starts the action with a corner kick that should be directed toward a zone near the far side of the goal area. At the same time, a player from Group B runs

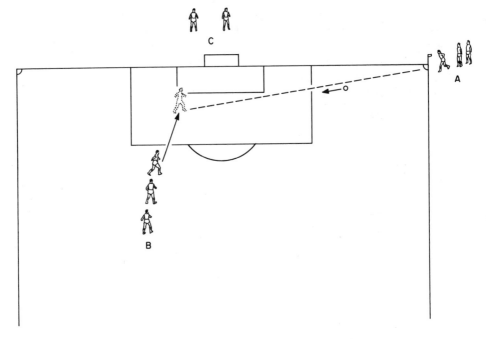

Fig. 4–13.   Corner kick drill.

toward the goal area and times his approach for a shot at goal. Whenever possible, the attacker should attempt to head the ball into the goal.

A player should always be assigned to sub-station C, to retrieve the ball in case it is kicked past or over the goal. As soon as the player from Group B completes his attempt at the goal, the players from the three sub-stations should rotate their positions and other players should repeat the drill. To simulate actual game conditions, additional players should be added to the drill, including a goalkeeper and other defenders.

The *penalty kick drill* gives players opportunities to practice what is, perhaps, the game's most crucial situation, a free shot at the goal from a distance of 12 yards. The penalty kick situation is governed by the laws of the game; consequently, the drill should stress the rules involved.

STATION TEN (FOUR-ON-TWO DRILL)

The *four-on-two drill* stresses trapping, passing, tackling, and teamwork. The object of the drill is for four players to keep the ball away from two defenders. The movements of the players should be restricted to a designated zone, and the attackers should be required to maintain positions that surround the defenders. (See Fig. 4–14.)

To give all the players opportunities to benefit from all aspects of the drill, the defender who touches or gains possession of the ball should switch assignments with the attacker who last played it. To make it more difficult for the attackers, certain conditions should

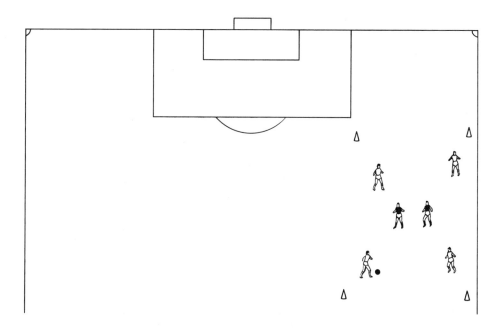

Fig. 4–14. Four-on-two drill.

be attached to the drill. For example, a condition for the four attackers might be one that restricts movement of the ball to first-time passing.

STATION ELEVEN

1. Informal Scrimmages
2. Pressure Defense Drill

Informal scrimmages involving five, six, or seven on each side give players more opportunities to play the ball than they ordinarily get when performing in an actual game. In addition the scrimmages are excellent physical fitness drills.

The area across half of the field of play is recommended for staging a scrimmage that involves a limited number of players. Designate the mid-field line and the goal line as touch lines, the regular touch lines as goal lines, and improvise goals by using towels, soccer jerseys, or the rubber-coned street markers mentioned earlier in this chapter.

If the coach wants to stress certain skills or parts of the game, certain conditions should be attached to the scrimmage, such as: short passing only, first-time passing only, etc.

Gradually, training should progress from scrimmages that stress parts of the game to sessions designed to give players opportunities to apply their skills, tactics, and physical fitness to the whole game. The *pressure defense drill* is a step in this direction, as it stresses the patterns of the game that develop in and around the penalty area. This is the area of the field that is the most crucial for both the defense and the offense.

The number of players involved in the pressure defense drill should vary according to the strategy that is being stressed. Generally, a goalkeeper, two fullbacks, and a center halfback constitute the defense and five forwards and a halfback make up the offense. If a fourth back is used in the drill, an additional halfback should be added to the attackers. (See Fig. 4–15.) The object of the drill is for the offense, with a numerical advantage, to maintain a continuous attack against the defenders.

The conditions for the pressure defense drill are as follows: play is limited to one half of the field; whenever the defense gains possession of the ball, it must clear it immediately to the opposing halfback who, in turn, must start another attack without delay; when it is to its advantage, the defense should use off-side tactics; the attackers should stress pressure tactics in their attempts to create two-on-one or three-on-two situations; and, if the need arises, the offense should pass the ball back to the halfback for support.

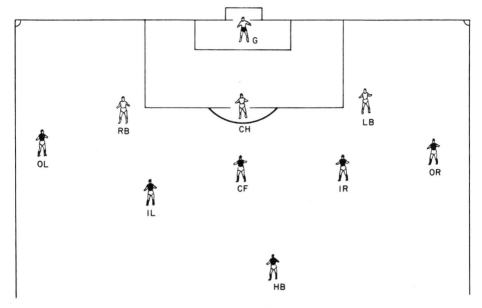

Fig. 4–15. The pressure defense drill stresses the patterns of the game that develop in and around the penalty area.

STATION TWELVE

1. Double Duty Scrimmage
2. Controlled Scrimmage

The *double duty scrimmage* is a training method which continues progression toward a full-scale game. To organize the scrimmage, each side should be assigned a goalkeeper, two fullbacks, and three halfbacks. In addition, one five-man forward line is involved in the following manner: during the course of the scrimmage, the forward line must play on the side of the team that last clears the ball across the mid-field line. Thus the forwards serve as teammates for a side as long as the ball is in the opponents' half of the field. However, if the opposition clears the ball back across the mid-field line, the forwards must immediately become a part of that side. The key to the scrimmage is to keep the ball in the other team's territory.

To distinguish the three groups of players, use different colored jerseys. The scrimmage should be started by arbitrarily assigning the forward line to one of the sides. (See Fig. 4–16.)

The double duty scrimmage is an excellent method for training both the offense and defense. The defenders are placed in a

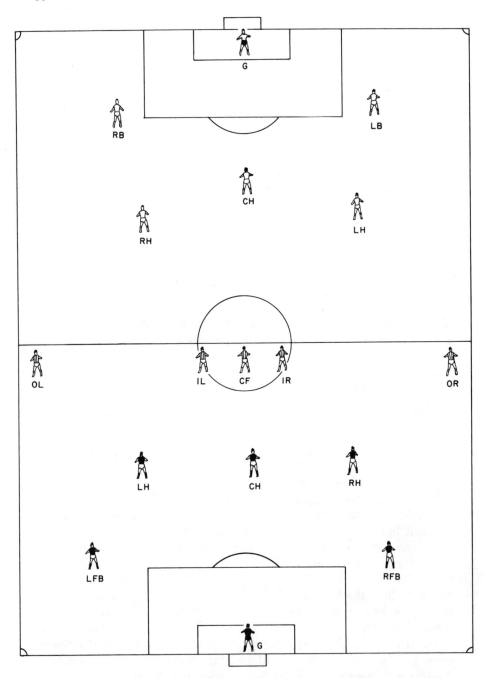

Fig. 4–16. In the double duty scrimmage, the forward line plays on the side of the team that last clears the ball across the mid-field line.

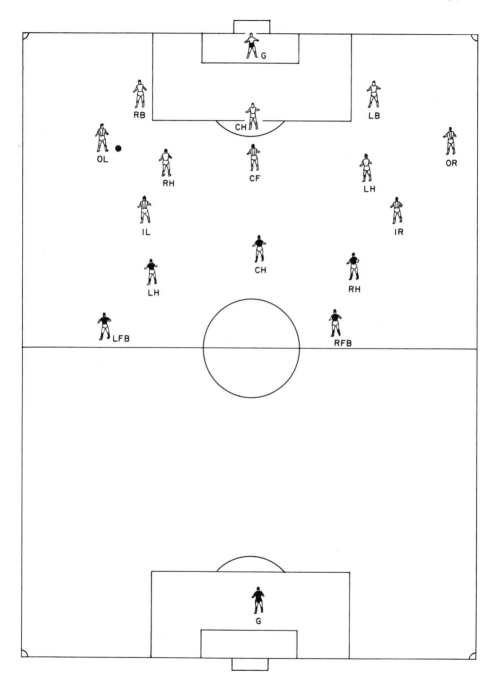

Fig. 4–17. The double duty scrimmage stresses total team involvement.

Fig. 4—18.   Power training for soccer-football (copyright Raoul Mollet, CISM).

pressure situation, because they are outnumbered by the offense and, at the same time, the forwards have an opportunity to develop their physical and skill training by working with both teams. In addition, it teaches the defenders the importance of total team involvement in the attacking phase of the game. In order to keep the ball in the opponents' half of the field, the halfbacks and fullbacks must move up to support the forward line. (See Fig. 4–17.)

Once players have had opportunities to develop their skills and improve their fitness, they should participate in *controlled scrimmages* involving two full sides. A controlled scrimmage is a game-type training situation. During the scrimmage, game conditions should apply, with the exception of interruptions of play for rule interpretations or explanations of individual tactics and game strategy. At the opportune time, play may also be stopped to discuss the various relevant aspects of the scrimmage. The controlled scrimmage should be the culmination of the training program.

POWER TRAINING

To insure total fitness for the game of soccer, many programs allocate a portion of the training session on a daily or periodical basis to an exercise program that is specifically designed to improve muscular fitness and endurance. This phase of the program has been designated by some authorities as "Power Training for Soccer." Basically, it is a circuit program that includes weight training and other exercises that can contribute to the physical fitness needed for soccer. The circuit arrangement works in the interest of time, by using an organizational pattern that minimizes periods of delay and lost motion that are common to many training sessions. For best results, the circuit exercise program should be used in conjunction with the drills and training techniques previously described in this chapter.

A well-known advocate of power training for sports is Major Raoul Mollet, Secretary General of The International Military Sports Council, Brussels, Belgium. The following is his concept of what constitutes a power training program for soccer. (See Fig. 4–18.)[2]

SITE FOR POWER TRAINING

A gymnasium, hall, or room adjacent to the practice field is recommended as the site for establishing a power training circuit. The indoor facility is especially suited to the needs of a soccer

[2] Mollet, Raoul, "Power Training" (Brussels: Conseil International du Sport Militaire Magazine, 1960).

program that is conducted during periods of inclement weather. In addition, it provides an air of permanency for the players, a meeting place that affords them opportunities to expend the extra efforts needed to enhance their personal development as well as their team morale.

The power training site includes space needed to conduct warm-up exercises, an area for a series of power exercises, and space for the phase of the circuit that is devoted to stretching exercises. To administer the program, provision should be made for a command post, or staging center, which includes: an office or appropriate space for filing individual cards and other paper work; and a bulletin board for posting pertinent materials, such as photographs, drawings, descriptions of exercises, faults to avoid, safety precautions, etc.

The installation of a power training circuit requires:

1. The assembly of the necessary equipment.
2. The establishment of a series of exercises, including:
   a. Seven warm-up exercises.
   b. A series of eighteen power exercises.
   c. Four stretch exercises.
   d. Individual exercise cards.

EQUIPMENT

The minimum equipment required for six athletes exercising at the same time includes:

1. Five weight-training bars with a free play of weights.
2. Two pairs of two pound dumbbells.
3. Two twelve-pound medicine balls.
4. Four tumbling mats.
5. Two small exercise mats.
6. One fixed wooden or concrete step—2″ × 16″ × 16″.
7. Four track hurdles.
8. One stationary wall target.
9. A suspended ball apparatus.
10. Two or more skip ropes.
11. One set of stall bars.
12. Two sets of ankle weights.
13. One exercise board with ankle straps.
14. One vaulting box.
15. Thirty markers.

THE CIRCUIT

The circuit is planned for a duration of thirty minutes, and it is organized in the following manner:

1. Warm-up exercises—5 minutes.
2. Power exercises—20 minutes.
3. Stretch exercises—3 minutes.
4. Relaxation—2 minutes.

To warm up the large muscle groups used in soccer, the players should perform three to five of the exercises illustrated in Figure 4–18. The movements for each exercise should be done in a rhythm-like fashion, with or without the use of two pound weights, for a period of one minute. Once the warm-up begins, the players should not stop between exercises.

The *power series* includes eighteen exercises; however, the recommended cycle for each player is ten to twelve exercises. The higher number allows for some individual choice and permits a balance: five weight training exercises, four exercises with light weights, six elementary acrobatic exercises, and one sit-up exercise.

It is essential for the athletes to be familiar with all the exercises. To avoid confusion, the exercises should be numbered and placed in a well-determined order. Sample drawings or photographs should be suspended near the areas designated for the power series. For a psychological effect, pictures of well-known soccer players should be used.

Once the athlete has completed his warm-up exercises, he begins his power series according to the order and instructions indicated on his personal card. If the athlete is not thoroughly familiar with an exercise, he should refer to the numbered exercise and the informational material that is posted in the designated areas. The player should check to see that the necessary equipment is in place. When using weights the athlete should check to see that the weight corresponds to that prescribed on his personal card. Once the player completes the prescribed number of repetitions, he should move into position for the next exercise. The time between exercises should allow for 10–20 seconds of muscular relaxation.

The power training circuit ends with the players executing the four stretch exercises illustrated in Figure 4–18. At the end of the stretch exercises, the players move on to the practice field for the soccer training session.

The coach should be in charge of the power training circuit at all times. He should verify the executions, correct faults, and help maintain an atmosphere that is conducive to a voluntary workout.

To determine the individual formula for each of his players, the coach should maintain a training manual or a permanent file to record the strengths and weaknesses of his players. This information is usually based on previous power training sessions, observations on the field of play, and a testing program that uses a back and leg dynamometer to measure the power or muscular force exerted by individual players. On the basis of all available information, the coach outlines a power training routine for a player by selecting ten to twelve exercises from the series. Some of the exercises are assigned to improve weak points in an individual's muscular development and others to further strengthen the strong points, thus assuring a general power increase.

Planning the power training program is a question of individual proportioning. The coach must determine the amount of weight to be used and the number of repetitions. All this information should be recorded in each player's permanent file. Information regarding the number of exercises, weights, repetitions, etc. should be prepared on a smaller card and given to the player before each power training session.

5

Playing the Game

The success of a soccer team depends largely upon the ability of its players to use teamwork and individual effort in a manner that insures the best development of tactical opportunities. As a prerequisite for maximum individual and team effort, consider the psychological aspects of the game. The attitude with which players approach a system of play is very important. Players must not only know the duties and responsibilities of every position on the field but understand and respect the principles of attack and defense around which a system revolves. In soccer, as in all sport, there is no room for bickering, jealousy, backbiting, and star attitudes.

The assignment of players to the positions where they will be most effective is very important to any system of play. Defensive positions require speed, sure tackling, accuracy in kicking, and effective heading. Height is an asset for defense and should be considered. In some systems the ability to attack like a forward has become increasingly important to fullback play. Players who play the halfback positions must be able to tackle as strongly and surely as fullbacks. The halfback position also requires skillful dribbling, accurate passing, effective heading, and the ability to shoot. In short, a halfback must be able to defend, attack, and, when necessary, combine both duties. Forwards are expected to be excellent shooters, quick starters, fast runners, and clever with their feet. A forward should feel at home at any position on the front line, and he should be prepared to assume the functions of a halfback or fullback if the situation so requires. Height and strength are physical attributes that are important for goalkeeping. The position also requires quick reactions, agility, courage, and the instinct of knowing how, when, and where the ball is coming.

The proper positioning of players can be best achieved through experimentation. Players must be given opportunities to play various positions. Eventually they will find their best position and, in the meantime, they will have had opportunities to become acquainted with the duties and responsibilities of other positions on the field. This is important because of the stress modern soccer strategy places on total team involvement, on both offense and defense.

Once players have been assigned to their proper positions, the strategy of the sport calls for a balanced formation that is concerned with plans of action depending on positional play. Use a system of positioning that balances the field of play and enables players to put forth their best efforts, on both offense and defense, with an optimum expenditure of energy. In addition, allow for the degree of flexibility a formation needs to cope with the strengths and weaknesses of the opposition.

The following formations afford a wide variety of tactical maneuvers and have been widely adopted by teams throughout the world as the basis for their systems of play.

THE WM FORMATION

The WM formation (Fig. 5–1) balances the offense and defense by assigning the primary duty of attack to five forwards who are

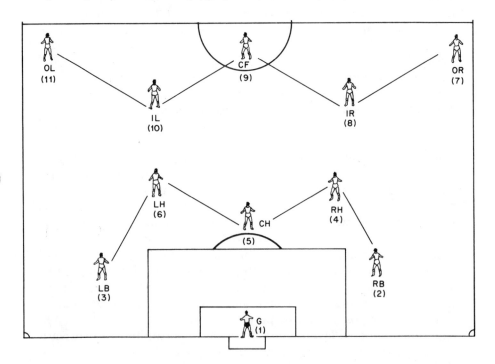

Fig. 5–1. WM formation.

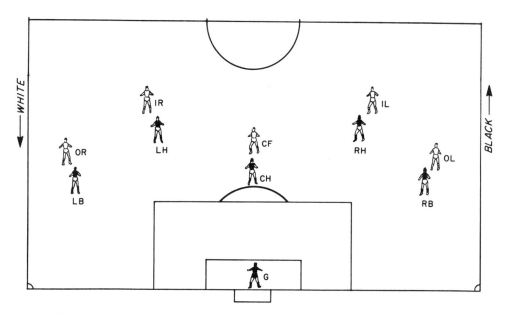

Fig. 5–2. Defensive assignments for the halfbacks and fullbacks in the WM formation.

positioned on the field of play in the shape of a W and the defense to five players who are positioned in the shape of an M. The five forwards include the center-forward, the two inside-forwards, and the two wingmen. The defense consists of two halfbacks, two fullbacks, a center-halfback, and the goalkeeper.

In the W phase of the formation, the center-forward and the two outside men lead the attack while the inside-forwards trail slightly behind. The inside-forwards act as playmakers for the center-forward, and the two wings quite often move into the front line for attempts at the goal. In addition, the inside-forwards drop back on defense to help the halfbacks. Although the center-forward and two wingmen are primarily concerned with attack, they must immediately go on defense when they are close to an opponent who has gained possession of the ball. When the center-forward and the wingmen are not involved in trying to take the ball away from their opponents, they position themselves around the mid-field line to receive the ball from their defense for a counter attack.

In the M phase of the formation, the two halfbacks play behind the inside-forwards and ahead of the fullback line. The halfbacks mark the opposing inside-forwards and act as extra backs, when needed. On offense they support the forward line and quite often become directly involved as extra forwards.

The two fullbacks, along with the center-halfback, play behind and parallel to the halfbacks. The fullbacks mark the opposing wings, or switch defensive assignments with the halfbacks to mark the opposing inside-forwards. The center-halfback, who plays what is often referred to as the center-fullback or stopper position, marks the opposing center-forward on defense. The three backs and two halfbacks coordinate their defensive duties by switching positions or covering for each other whenever the need arises. (See Fig. 5–2.)

THE 4–2–4 FORMATION

The 4–2–4 system of play (Fig. 5–3) evolved as attempts were made to correct and exploit the defensive weaknesses of the WM formation. The four-back system makes it more difficult to penetrate the approach to the goal. At the same time, the four backs allow for more flexibility and freedom of movement on the part of the four forwards and two halfbacks, as a counter attack by the opposition is not apt to outnumber the defense. In addition, a four-man defensive line, spread across the width of the field, allows for closer support for the forward line, and it places a back in a better position to immediately mark an opponent who has the ball.

To line up for the 4–2–4 formation, use four forwards, two halfbacks, and four fullbacks. The goalkeeper plays basically the same as in any other formation. The forward line consists of two wingmen, the center-forward, and one of the inside-forwards who moves up into the forward line as a double center-forward. The other inside-forward and one of the halfbacks play in the zone between the forward and defensive lines. The defensive line stretches across the width of the field, with two backs playing near the touch lines and the other two covering the center of the field.

During a game the positions and movements of the forwards depend upon the strategy of the attack and the defensive alignment of the opponents. The strategy may call for the four forwards to play in a line, for the wings to trail the two middle forwards, or for one or both center-forwards to trail the wingmen. If the opposing fullbacks use close man-to-man marking, it is good strategy for the wings to trail, as it affords opportunities for the middle forwards to break into open spaces behind the fullbacks or it opens a space for one of the halfbacks to move into the front line as an extra forward. (See Fig. 5–4.)

The tactics involving two middle forwards can be very effective against a formation using one center-fullback, particularly if the

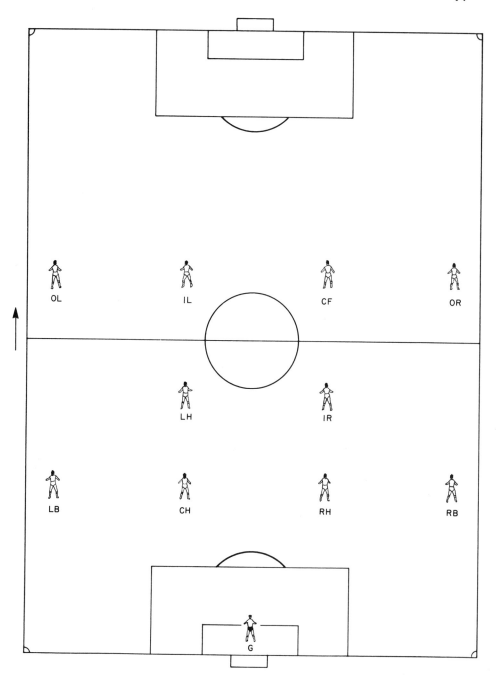

Fig. 5–3.   The 4–2–4 formation.

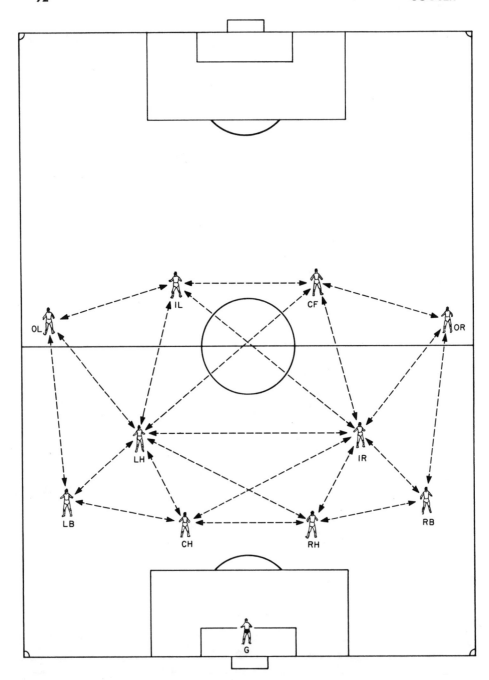

Fig. 5–4. The 4–2–4 allows for many variations. Occasionally the wings trail two forwards who attack as double center-forwards.

center-fullback is the lone defender in the middle of the field and is using close man-to-man marking against the center-forward. To open a space for a fast-breaking teammate, use the center-forward to decoy the center-fullback away from the approach to the goal.

On defense, the two fullbacks playing on the flanks of the defensive line mark the opposing wingmen, and the two middle backs cover opponents who spearhead the attack. The two halfbacks act as defenders in the area of the field between the defensive and forward lines and, whenever needed, they move back to assist their fullbacks. The forwards switch to defense immediately, if possession of the ball is lost in their immediate area or if it is to their team's tactical advantage for them to move back to assist the halfbacks or fullbacks.

THE 4–3–3 FORMATION

To line up for the 4–3–3 formation (Fig. 5–5) use four fullbacks, three halfbacks, and three forwards. The defensive line is the same as in the 4–2–4 formation. The middle line includes a halfback, a

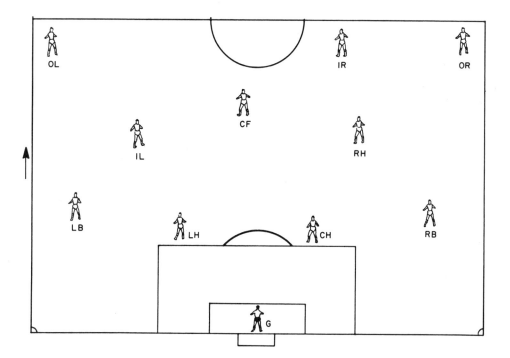

Fig. 5–5.   The 4–3–3 formation.

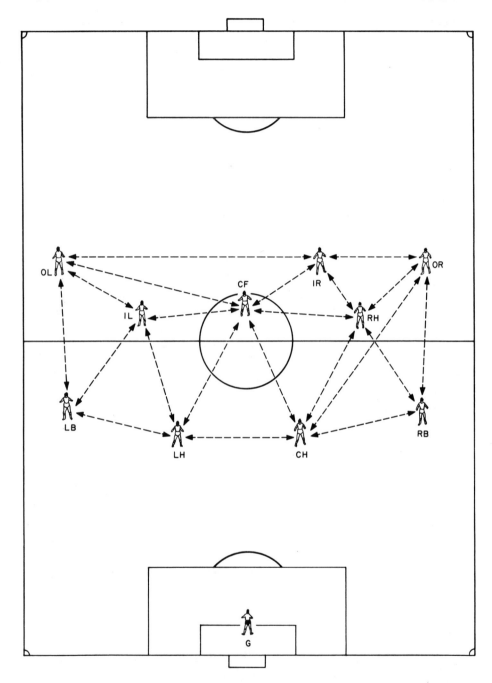

Fig. 5–6.   The 4–3–3 formation lends itself to a variety of pass patterns.

deep-lying center-forward, and an inside-forward. The forward line consists of two wingmen and the other inside-forward.

The deep-lying center-forward acts as a playmaker and helps the halfbacks on defense. He is also positioned to make quick moves into the forward line or to switch positions with a teammate. The relative positioning of the players in the 4–3–3 formation allows for a variety of pass patterns. (See Fig. 5–6.) On offense, the players positioned between the forward and defensive lines become directly involved as extra forwards and the defensive line moves up to support the attack.

PRINCIPLES OF ATTACK

The attacking phase of the game involves the skills and tactics that enable a side, through individual and team effort, to move the ball toward and into the opponents' goal. This is the object of the game. However, this does not imply that attack is concerned solely with tactics that move the ball forward. The nature of the game is such that a team cannot, as a rule, sustain a successful attack toward the opposing goal by exclusively emphasizing forward movements.

The defense enjoys certain advantages: the off-side rule; the handling of the ball by the goalkeeper in the penalty area; and tactical positioning that usually keeps the defenders between the attackers and the goal. In addition, a player without the ball can usually overtake a player with the ball and, in many situations, a defender has the opportunity to run to meet the ball for a quick head play or clearance kick. On the other hand, the attacker is usually playing under pressure of the time needed to control and move the ball with either a pass or shot. At this stage of the game, he is usually vulnerable to a quick tackle by a defender. To offset the advantages of the defense, the attack must consider a wide variety of maneuvers, and players must develop the ability to anticipate situations and opportunities that afford the best scoring possibilities.

As a rule the plan for an attack begins to develop even before a team gains possession of the ball. Players not directly involved with defense must position themselves for a counter attack and, at the same time, all the players must get into the habit of observing exactly where their teammates are, so that they can send the ball when one of their own side is in a good position to receive it. Modern soccer strategy calls for an attack in depth that is built around the movements of players with or without the ball; movements that are lateral, diagonal, and linear in range. To attack with a straight line of players across the field is poor strategy, as a single defender can immobilize the whole line by taking possession of the ball. An attack needs support that comes through proper positioning and complete team involvement. It is best accomplished through triangle patterns that enable players to combine their efforts to outnumber the defense by cutting through, behind, or ahead of opposing defenders into open spaces for pass receptions.

Once a player gains possession of the ball, the question of how long he controls it with a dribble depends upon whether or not one of his teammates is in a position to receive it for further progress toward the opponents' goal. Then, too, if a player is in danger of losing the ball, he must pass it quickly to a teammate who is in the open.

When an attack is initiated from a player's own half of the field, the strategy usually calls for quick passes with little or no dribbling. This especially holds true, if a fast break is in order. A dribble in one's own side of the field usually gives the opposition enough time to recover and to consolidate its defense. On occasion a player must dribble to avoid an opponent or while he is waiting for one of his teammates to get open for a pass. A dribble is sometimes used on the opponents' side of the field to draw out a defender. It is also used to give a teammate time to break into an open space or when a player has an opportunity for an individual effort toward the goal. However, a player should not get in the habit of dribbling too much. Sustained dribbling increases the chances of losing the ball, it detracts from teamwork, and quite often hurts team morale.

THE PASSING GAME

In modern soccer, passing has developed into the most important phase of the game. Without a sound passing game, it is virtually impossible for a team to cope with the formations and defenses currently being used. The passing game involves long and short passes. Many teams develop their offense around pass patterns that emphasis a long- or short-passing game or a combination of the two. The long-passing game is usually associated with fast-breaking maneuvers that attempt to spring a forward into an open space behind a back. Quite often a fast break starts with a long clearance kick or throw from the goalkeeper. (See Fig. 5–7.) When using the long pass as part of the fast break, aim at putting the ball in a space in front of the forward, so that the latter can take the ball on the run. When a forward has to wait for the ball to come to him, it gives the opposing defenders the advantage they need. The long

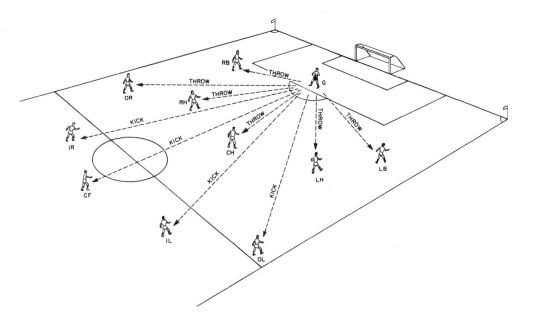

Fig. 5–7. The goalkeeper has a number of pass options when clearing the ball.

pass is also used as a means of spreading the defense. Quite often, when the defense is unbalanced or displaced, players on the opposite side of the field are open for a long cross pass. This is usually the strategy behind wing-to-wing play. One of the dangers of a long pass downfield is that the ball might be lost to the opposing defenders or goalkeeper. Consequently, most of the long passes are made along the touch line to a fast-breaking wing, or the ball is kept out of the goalkeeper's reach by using long diagonal passes to the forwards.

The short-passing attack requires perfect ball control. This style of play has been developed to perfection by many Latin American countries. The strategy of the short-passing game is to make progress toward the opposing goal by means of a series of passes and inter-passes that keep the defenders outnumbered and off-balance. (See Fig. 5–8.)

Unless a team has perfect touch with the ball, the short-passing style of attack has limited value because it gives the opposing defenders too many opportunities to stop an attack. Then, too, it

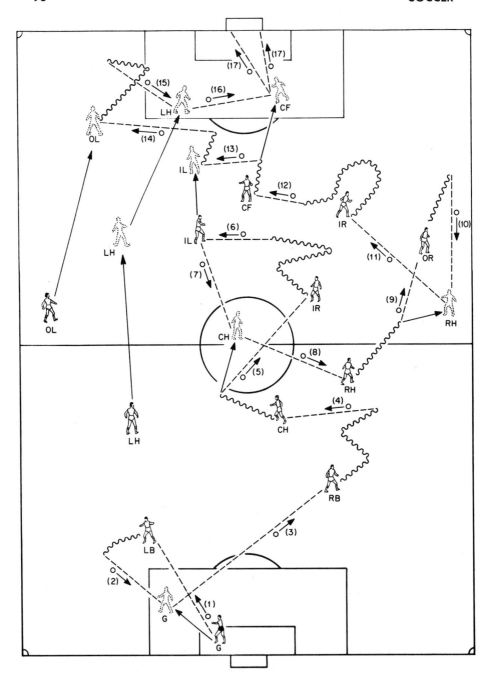

Fig. 5–8. The short-passing attack requires perfect ball control and tactics that keep the defenders off balance.

generally allows sufficient time for the opposing defenders to recover to form a strong defense around their penalty area.

Most soccer authorities agree that the best attack is one that uses a combination of long- and short-pass patterns. A varied attack allows for the flexibility needed to profit from tactical opportunities that develop during the course of a game. An attack that becomes stereotyped lacks imagination and makes the job for the opposing defenders much easier.

To develop successful pass patterns, there are certain elements that must be considered in addition to passing technique. Actually, passing technique is worthless unless there is a teammate open to receive the ball. Successful pass patterns depend upon simple tactics on the part of the passer, the receiver, and other teammates who can contribute to the development of the play. Use the following tactics to develop pass patterns.

SWITCHING TACTICS

The formations covered in this chapter lend themselves to horizontal movements and switching tactics as a means of developing pass patterns. For a pass play in which players change positions, the center-forward runs toward the touch line and into an open

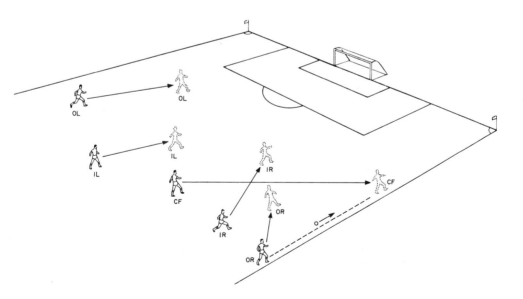

Fig. 5–9. Switching tactics for attacking forwards.

space ahead of a wingman who has control of the ball; the inside-forward, next to the wingman with the ball, runs ahead and into the center of the field; and the wingman takes the inside-forward's position, after passing the ball along the touch line into the open space ahead of the center-forward. The center-forward receives the ball on the run and, if unopposed, dribbles towards the opponents' goal in an attempt to score. If he is marked by a defender, he passes or centers the ball to one of his teammates. (See Fig. 5–9.)

A scissors movement between a wingman and an inside-forward can be a very effective tactical maneuver. The inside-forward sprints out to the wing and the wingman pushes the ball forward and then cuts inside to be in position to receive a return pass. (See Fig. 5–10.) In another scissors movement, the outside-left turns

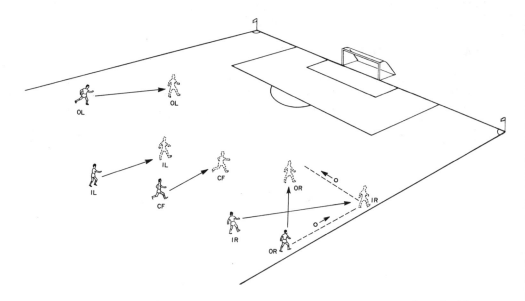

Fig. 5–10. A scissors movement between a wingman and an inside-forward.

inside with the ball and the inside-left cuts behind him towards the touchline to receive a pass. (See Fig. 5–11.) Scissors movements for pass plays are most effective when used near the wings because the touch line can be used to advantage.

THROUGH-PASS PATTERN

When opposing defenders restrict the pass possibilities to the smallest of spaces, or when they are employing off-side tactics, use

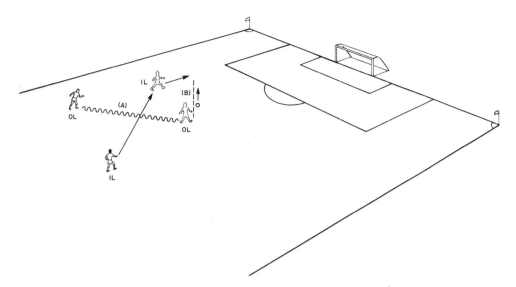

Fig. 5–11.   A scissors movement for a pass play.

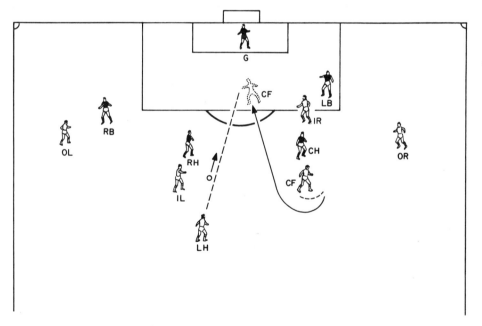

Fig. 5–12.   A through-pass pattern.

a through pass to a teammate. To execute the through pass, push the ball forward between two defenders to a teammate, who fakes his opponent and breaks for the ball at full speed. This can be an excellent maneuver for an attempt at goal, and it is used quite often in and around the penalty area. (See Fig. 5–12.)

RETURN-PASS PATTERN

Return-pass patterns are tactics that are common to an attack that stresses total team involvement. The strategy of the return pass is for the passer to stay with the attack by running to an open space. This maneuver not only results in numerous pass openings, but it keeps pressure on the opposing defenders, as they must continue to concentrate their defensive efforts against the player who has passed the ball, as well as the receiver. When a return pass pattern is used to set up a shot at goal, it is commonly referred to as the give-and-go, or the old one-two. (See Fig. 5–13.)

The strategy associated with return pass patterns points up the importance and need for close support for a player with the ball. To avoid situations that leave players stranded with the ball and to capitalize on the opportunities afforded by close support to the man with the ball, stress complete team involvement in a depth attack.

PRESSURE SOCCER

The strategy behind pressure soccer is for the team to set a pace throughout the course of the game which the opponents are not physically prepared to handle. A team that is physically tired is obviously more vulnerable to attack. A pressure style of play demands a high degree of fitness by all members of a team and collective tactics that will use it to best advantage.

For pressure soccer, train players to be quick on the ball, both on offense and defense. Whenever possible use a fast break that starts with a quick clearance by the goalkeeper. On throw-ins, goal kicks, or fouls, put the ball back into play without delay. Keep a steady pressure and concentrate the attack on the opposing defenders who show weaknesses or signs of fatigue.

PRINCIPLES OF DEFENSE

The defense is concerned with preventing the opposition from scoring and, at the same time, regaining possession of the ball so that its own offense will have an opportunity to score. The key to the game of soccer is ball control; once the ball is lost to the opposition, it must be regained.

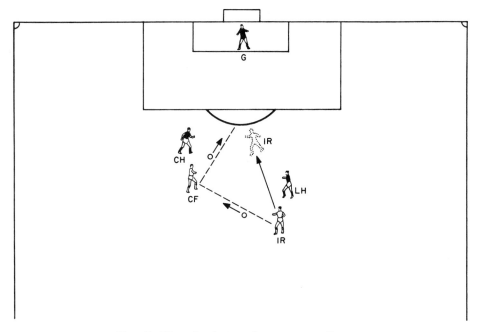

Fig. 5–13.   A give-and-go pass pattern.

Although certain positions are more concerned with defense than others, every player on the team has an obligation toward the defense, if the situation warrants it.   Alertness on the part of every player will quite often enable a team to regain possession of the ball at the most opportune time.   A sound defense also requires a thorough knowledge of the various formations, skills, and strategies common to the game.   Insight into the game helps defenders assume positions in relation to the flow of the game which quite often offset certain moves by the offense.   To develop a sound defense, combine these factors with a complete mastery of all the defensive skills.

POSITIONING

During the course of a game, players constantly maneuver for positions that give them advantages needed for the performance of their duties.   Defenders must be prepared to adapt to the formation and tactics of the attack, as well as movements that are unexpected or do not fall within set patterns of play.   This includes maneuvers designed to confuse the defense—drawing defenders out of position, switching tactics, and lateral or diagonal movements. As a rule, defenders maintain positions slightly behind and between the attackers and the goal, while attackers, with or without the ball, attempt to move into spaces behind the defenders. The movements of the offense are restricted somewhat by the off-side rule, which does not permit an attacker to run behind a defender unless the ball is ahead of the attacker, or he has at least two defenders between himself and the goal at the moment the ball is played forward by one of his teammates. When used properly, the off-side rule is a definite advantage for the defense. On the other hand, the attack controls the ball and has the element of surprise in its favor.

The distance a defender maintains from an attacker depends on a number of factors: where on the field the ball is being played; whether or not the zone for which he is responsible is likely to become immediately involved with an ensuing attack; the speed of an attacker; the dribbling ability of an attacker; a player's overall ability; and opportunities for interceptions.

When the ball is not in the immediate vicinity, use a swivel-type rotation to move toward and behind the zone where the ball is being played to cover for a teammate or guard against a possible breakthrough toward the goal.

Around the penalty area use man-to-man marking against the offense and tight coverage on the player who has the ball. Mark the attacker who has the ball immediately and be prepared to use the side of either foot to smother an attempted shot at goal. Whenever possible, clear the ball away from the goal and toward the touch line without delay. A sound principle in defense is to direct clearances toward the touch lines. A pass or clearance directed toward the middle of the field or one that passes in front of the goal is poor strategy, as it affords opportunities for interceptions by the opponents and quite often puts them into position to score.

Against an attacker who has superior speed, it is best not to use close marking unless the attacker has possession of the ball or is without the ball but in a position that constitutes a definite threat to the goal. Instead, use a zone defense or loose marking, which will not give an attacker the opportunity to use his superior speed to get behind the defense. The same strategy applies against an opponent who is a clever dribbler. If the dribbler has control of the ball, keep a distance that will not permit him to break through and away. Use harassment tactics and play for an interception. However, if a clever dribbler is threatening the goal, the defense must use tight coverage. Whenever possible, use double coverage against a clever dribbler by coordinating defensive efforts with a teammate.

A team with a star offensive performer presents a special problem. To nullify the threat of an outstanding playmaker or scorer, assign a defender, usually a halfback, the task of shadowing the player in question throughout the game. If the opponents play the ball to their key player, the defender must be in position for a possible interception or a quick tackle. If the star performer gets control of the ball, the defender must use tight coverage and make it difficult for the player with the ball to develop a play or otherwise use his superior ability. As a rule, a player who is constantly shadowed tends to get discouraged and, at the same time, it frustrates his teammates and their planned attack.

Proper positioning, along with the ability to anticipate the moves of the opposition, quite often leads to interceptions that can be turned into quick counter attacks. To be ready for possible interceptions, defenders must develop an awareness that keeps them alert to the strategy of the game at all times. On defense always move toward the area where the ball is being played and into a position that affords the best possibility for an interception. At the same time, be aware of the movements of opposing attackers who are most likely to get a pass from the player with the ball. If the anticipated play develops, beat the pass receiver to the ball or, if possible, cut off the intended pass.

DEFENSIVE SWITCHING

Soccer is a game of checks, balances, and counterbalances. Many attacking forwards attempt to confuse the defense by switching positions. To keep from being outmaneuvered by the attack, defenders adjust to the situation by either following the attackers into their new positions or by switching defensive assignments with a teammate. The latter method calls for a defense that is responsible for zones rather then individual opponents, and in many situations is the only effective strategy for dealing with forwards who are constantly changing positions. For example, it is common practice for an opposing center-forward to run toward the touch line in an effort to decoy the center-halfback away from the middle of the field. The defending center-halfback counters the strategy of the attack with the help of his fullback, who marks the opposing center-forward as he moves toward the touch line. As a result, the center-halfback remains in his zone to guard against a possible breakthrough by one of the opposing center-forward's teammates.

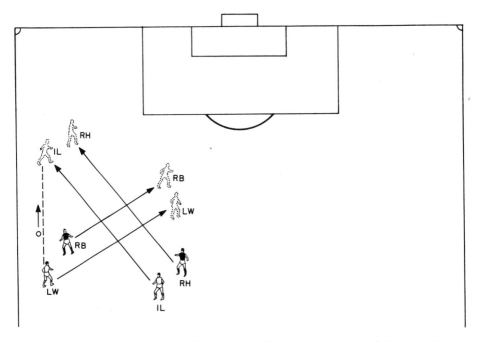

Fig. 5–14. Quite often defenders will counter an attack by switching defensive positions.

In some situations it is to the defenders' advantage to switch right along with their opponents, especially if the switching movements occur near the touch line. In Fig. 5–14 the left wingman switches into the inside-forward's position after passing the ball down the touch line to the inside-left, who has now assumed the wingman's position. At the same time, the defending right back switches right along with the outside-left and the right-halfback moves out toward the wing with the inside-left. The defenders stay in their new positions until the threat has passed or the ball is played away from their zone.

GOALKEEPING

While mistakes by players other than the goalkeeper do not necessarily pose a threat to their goal, a miscue by the goalie often results in a score for the opposition. Consequently, successful goalkeeping allows for little or no margin of error. It is a position that must be played with detailed perfection and nothing can be left to chance. To be a successful goalkeeper, master the goal-tending skills covered in Chapter 3 and know how and when to relate them to the movement of the ball and the strategy of the game.

In order for each defender to know exactly what to do and what not to do when there is a threat to the goal, there must be complete understanding between the goalkeeper and his backs. Inasmuch as the goalkeeper is facing the impending attack, he is in better position and usually has more time to evaluate the situation. Therefore, the goalie is the logical player to direct the play of the defenders in and around the penalty area. The goalkeeper should keep his teammates alert to gaps in the defense and give calls for certain moves by the defenders.

On occasion, a defender is in a situation where he is running toward his own goal after a loose ball and has an opponent at his heels. Under such conditions, the defender risks a possible interception if he turns with the ball. To avoid a possible interception, play the ball back to the goalkeeper for a clearance kick or throw. To execute this play, the goalkeeper and back communicate their intentions and the ball is passed back to the goalie in a manner that will not pose a threat to the goal. Note in Fig. 5–15 that the goal-

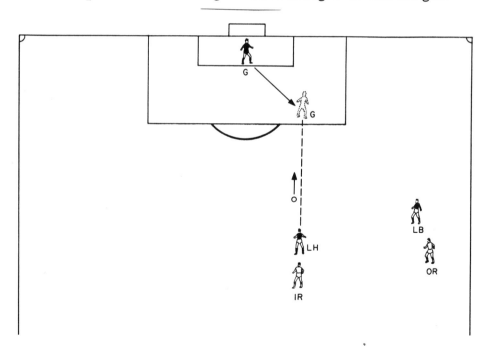

Fig. 5–15. In certain situations, the strategy calls for a defender to play the ball back to his goalkeeper.

keeper has moved up in the penalty area to receive the ball from his left-halfback who is being harassed by the opposing inside-right.

The goalkeeper uses various methods for dealing with shots at goal: catching, fisting, tipping the ball over the cross-bar, and kicking the ball without the use of the hands. Catching the ball is generally the safest method and, whenever possible, the ball should be caught with both hands. In order to be able to dispose of the ball in an effective manner, the goalkeeper should get into the habit of observing exactly where the players are so that without hesitation he can clear the ball to one of his own side who is in a good position to receive it. When there is time, a long punt or drop kick toward the sideline is considered good strategy, as it gains the most ground and is likely to go out of the normal range of play of the opposing defensive players. Another method for clearing the ball is a throw to a teammate who is unmarked and positioned to continue offensive play.

When the ball cannot be caught or has to be cleared rapidly, the goalkeeper relies on fisting, tipping, or kicking techniques. To react successfully to a fisting or tipping situation, the goalkeeper uses reflex-like patterns which have been developed through previous practice and competition. As a rule the goalkeeper uses a kick to clear the ball when he cannot bend down to use his hands or when he has to play the ball when it is outside the penalty area.

In the final analysis, the basis for successful goal-tending is the goalkeeper's ability to read play situations. This calls for constant awareness and positioning while continuously adjusting to the movement of the ball. The goalkeeper determines his position in front of the goal in relation to the point on the field where the ball is being played and in a manner in which he can best deal with a shot at goal. The goalkeeper must know when or when not to move out to play the ball. If the goalkeeper has an opportunity to move towards the ball to field it just as it enters the penalty area, this should be his first option. On the other hand, if it is not to the goalkeeper's advantage to run to meet the ball, he must assume a position that will reduce the shooter's angle of possibility if a shot is taken. To narrow the shooting angle, face the kicker squarely and stand one to two yards in front of the goal at a point where an imaginary line bisects the angle of possibility for the shooter. (See Fig. 5–16.) Actually, the closer the goalkeeper moves toward the ball, the more it narrows the angle of possibility for the shooter. Of course, if the goalkeeper moves too far away from the goal, there is always the danger of a score by a shot lofted over his head. However, if the goalkeeper is the last line of defense and the attacker is

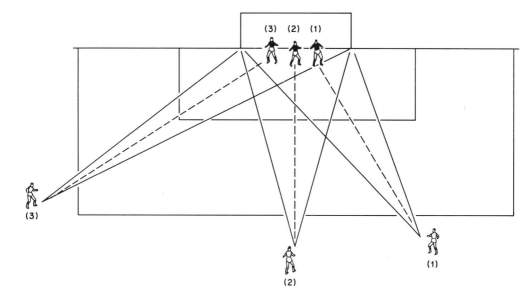

Fig. 5–16. Proper positioning by the goalkeeper will narrow the shooter's angle of possibility.

approaching the mouth of the goal, the goalkeeper must come out of the goal to meet the attacker and to counter the threat of a score.

GAME SITUATIONS

A situation during the course of a game is the state of affairs at any given moment. Actually, the game of soccer is a composite of many situations. Some situations result from the application of the laws of the game, for the rules not only influence but, in some cases, even govern the strategy of play. Other situations develop either through basic patterns of play that soccer circles have come to accept as sound strategy or through unique patterns that reflect the imaginations of creative and highly skilled players.

As players gain experience, they soon recognize that situations tend to repeat themselves during a game. Players also learn that some situations repeat themselves more than others and that some are more critical than others. Eventually soccer players instinctively sense tactical situations.

The following are situations that can be expected during a game.

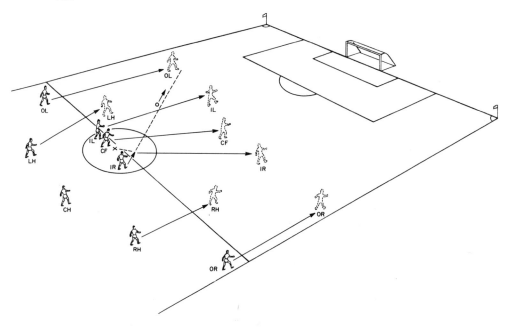

Fig. 5–17. Kick-off play to wing.

THE KICK-OFF

As the weather becomes a factor in the choice of ends, game strategy begins with the toss of the coin. If the wind, sun, or other climatic conditions favor one end of the field over the other, this should be considered when exercising the option of kicking off or choice of ends.[1]

The team taking the kick-off faces a difficult situation, as the attack is restricted by the rules that require each team to be in its own side of the field at the kick-off. The attack needs time to get players into the opponents' side of the field to act as possible pass receivers. At the same time, the defenders are all in their own side of the field in positions set for a strong defensive effort. To use the kick-off to advantage, use basic plays that enable teammates to move into the opponents' side of the field to put the attack in motion. Kick-off plays often involve fast-breaking wingmen who

---

[1] For detailed information covering the international rules for the kick-off and the punishment for any infringement thereof, the reader is referred to the rules of The United States Soccer Football Association. For interpretations of the rule in inter-collegiate, or interscholastic soccer, use The National Intercollegiate Athletic Associations Annual Soccer Guide.

play near the touch lines. For a kick-off play to a wingman, the center-forward touches the ball to one of his inside-forwards who, in turn, kicks the ball into a space ahead of a fast-breaking wingman. In the meantime, the other forwards move into the opponents' side of the field to support the attack. The play can be made to either wingman. This strategy is considered sound, as positions near the touch lines are usually not as cluttered with defenders. Then, too, a ball played to the wing tends to spread the defense, which creates openings for crosses into the middle of the field. It can be a very effective play for a team with fast wingmen. (See Fig. 5–17.)

Fig. 5–18 shows the defense for a kick-off play that sends the ball to the right wing. The defense starts with the defending center-forward and his inside forwards, who position themselves for a quick tackle or possible interception just as soon as the ball is kicked off. In the meantime, the defending fullbacks use loose man-to-man coverage against the wingmen until it is obvious to whom the pass is to be made. At this point, the defending left back moves toward the wingman for an interception or a quick tackle. If the defending left back is not able to prevent the outside-right from gaining possession of the ball, he must use close marking

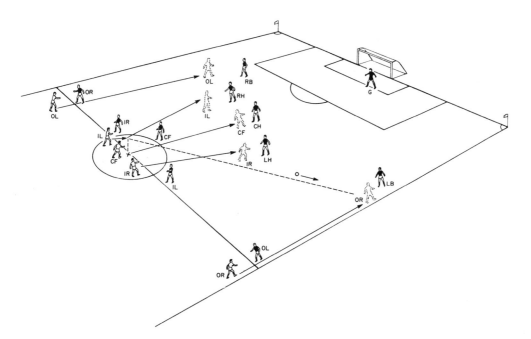

Fig. 5–18. Defensive assignments for a kick-off play to the wing.

and maintain a position that will keep him between the attacker and the goal. When the ball is played to the wing, the defending half-back line marks the attacking forwards who move into the defenders' side of the field to support their attack. Note that the half-back line pulls back to form a defensive line that is diagonal in relation to the position of the ball, and that the fullback defending the opposite side of the field moves slightly behind the diagonal line and toward the front of the goal. Diagonal alignment by the halfbacks and the positioning of the opposite fullback assures the defenders of mutual support and a defense in depth, in case of a possible breakthrough.

Many kick-off patterns get underway with a pass back to a half-back immediately after the ball is put into play. A pass back into a team's own side of the field not only rules out the likelihood of the opposing forwards obtaining possession of the ball, but it also serves as a delaying tactic that gives players from the attacking team time to move into open spaces in the opponents' side of the field. See Fig. 5–19 for a kick-off play that starts with the center-forward tapping the ball ahead of the inside-forward, who turns and passes

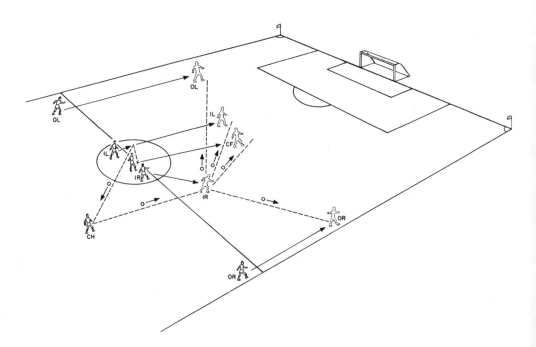

Fig. 5–19. A kick-off play with a pass back to the center-halfback.

it back to the center-halfback moving up to meet the ball. The center-halfback gains control of the ball in a situation that gives him time to observe the movements of his forwards and to select the best option for a pass. Pass possibilities for the center-halfback might include: a pass to the inside-forward who, in turn, passes the ball to one of the other forwards; a long pass to the center-forward breaking down the middle of the field; a long pass to a wingman; or a lateral pass to a halfback who moves up to take the pressure off the center-halfback. If pass opportunities ahead of the center-half-back fail to materialize and he is in danger of losing the ball, a pass back to one of the fullbacks will usually ease the pressure from the defense long enough for the offense to continue its efforts.

There are a variety of kick-off patterns, some more intricate then others. If a team is to use the kick-off to best advantage, it must pre-plan its strategy. When planning kick-off plays, consider whether or not the performance abilities of the players measure up to the degree of skill needed to make the plays work and select patterns that fit into the team's system of play.

THROWING IN

In the WM formation the responsibility for a throw-in is generally assigned to one of the halfbacks, except when the strategy calls for a fast play or when a team is awarded a throw-in deep in its opponents' territory. For a fast play, the attacker who can get to the ball first should throw it. In case of a throw-in situation deep in the opponents' side of the field, one of the forwards throws the ball while his teammates use switching tactics to balance their attack formation.

In other systems of play, the responsibility for the throw-in is assumed by any one of many players, depending on the tactics needed for a given situation. In the four-back defensive system, a fullback usually throws the ball when his team is awarded an out-of-bounds play in its own half of the field. However, when the attacking team is awarded a throw-in within the opponents' half of the field, a halfback or a forward is generally in the best position to execute the throw. It is important for forwards, halfbacks, and full-backs to all become proficient at throwing the ball, as a variety of throw-in situations occur quite often during the course of a game. To avoid a violation of the throw-in rule, follow the rule carefully and master the throw-in techniques described in Chapter 3.

The offensive and defensive strategy for the throw-in depends upon the score of the game and at what point on the touch line the ball is ruled out-of-bounds. When a team is behind on the score-board and playing against time, it is essential for the trailing team to complete their throw-ins with as little delay as possible. There are other situations when it is to either team's advantage to throw-in without delay: when the defense is off balance, or when a member of the attacking team is open and in position to profit by immediate possession of the ball. Both teams must be alert as to where the ball is ruled out-of-bounds and adjust their positions accordingly. When a throw-in play takes place in or close to the middle third of the field, the situation is not as critical for the defenders as it would be for one taken deep in their own territory. Fig. 5–20 shows a throw-in situation near the middle of the field. Note that the attacking team has four players: the outside-right, center-forward, inside-right, and the right back positioned within range of a throw-in, and that the defenders are marking them closely with the left back free to act as a sweeper in case of a breakthrough.

When the marking by the defense is so tight that a throw-in to a teammate is likely to be intercepted, the marked players must make every effort to break into open spaces. In a tight situation, a com-mon tactic is for an attacker to fake a quick move toward the op-ponents' goal and then suddenly reverse his direction to receive the ball for a play back to the thrower. The rules do not permit the thrower to play the ball a second time before it has been touched or played by another player. The ball should be thrown high enough to a teammate for a head play back to the thrower's feet, or it should be thrown in a manner that permits a player to use the inside of his foot for a pass back to the thrower. Players must co-ordinate their efforts by calling or signalling to each other.

It is possible to nullify the pass back play by assigning a defender to the thrower. In Fig. 5–21 the inside-left is marking the thrower, and the other defensive assignments are basically the same as in Fig. 5–20, except for the left-halfback, who now marks the at-tacking inside-right, and the left back, who marks the opposing out-side-right. This defensive arrangement eliminates the left back as a sweeper. In this situation, a player often throws the ball along the touch line and ahead of his wingman after the wingman has had an opportunity to fake a quick move forward and then reverse his direc-tion with a fast break. This play creates a potential scoring situa-tion, especially if the wingman gets behind his opponent and con-trols the ball on the run.

When a throw-in is taken by a team deep in its own territory, care must be taken against a possible miscue that might lead to a score by the opposition. The first option for the thrower should be a

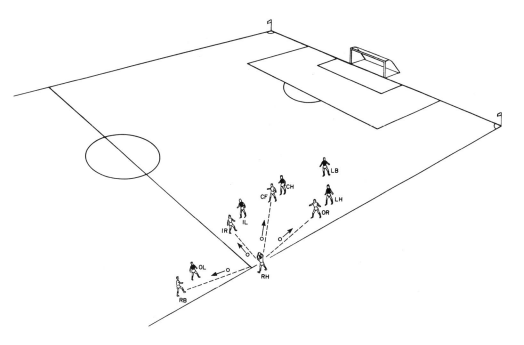

Fig. 5–20. Throw-in options and defensive assignments for a play near the middle of the field.

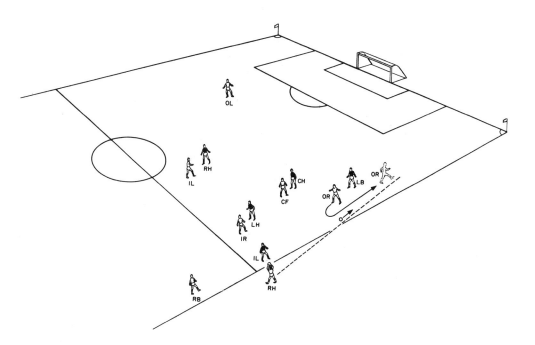

Fig. 5–21. Throw-in strategy when a defender is marking the thrower.

115

quick toss to the goalkeeper, who must call for the ball as he runs toward the edge of the penalty area. This creates a situation whereby the goalkeeper can handle the ball and start a counter attack with a long punt, drop kick, or throw to a teammate. The success of this play depends on the element of surprise, which hinges on quick moves by the thrower and his goalkeeper. (See Fig. 5–22.) To guard against this play, defenders often assign a teammate to mark the goalkeeper during a throw-in situation. Under such conditions, it is safer for a player to throw downfield to his wingman, who moves back to meet the ball. (See Fig. 5–23.)

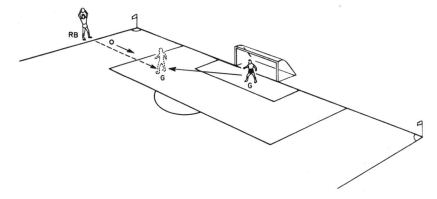

Fig. 5–22. A throw-in to the goalkeeper.

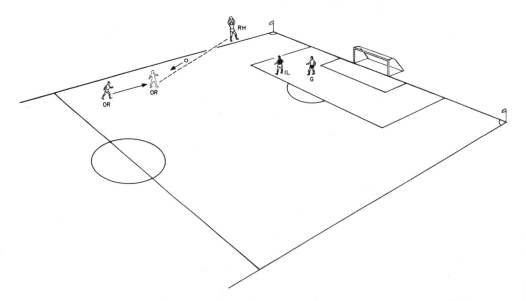

Fig. 5–23. Throw-in option when the goalkeeper is covered.

A throw-in by a team deep in the opponents' side of the field presents a scoring opportunity for the attacking team. In most cases the attacker nearest the ball when it goes out-of-bounds throws it back on to the field of play before the defense has time to get set, and it is not uncommon for a player to throw the ball to a teammate who is near the mouth of the goal. This situation also presents another special problem for the defense: the off-side rule is not in effect on a throw-in, which rules out the possibility of using off-side tactics to keep the attackers away from the goal. Under such conditions, the defenders must use tight man-to-man marking around every attacker who is in range of the throw-in, and they must make every effort to clear the ball away from the penalty area without delay.

GOAL KICK

The defenders are awarded a goal kick from their goal area when the ball completely crosses the goal line above or wide of the goal and is last played by the attacking team. The ball is kicked directly into play beyond the penalty area from a point within that half of the goal area nearest to where it crossed the line. The opponents are not allowed in the penalty area while the kick is being taken and the kicker is not permitted to touch the ball a second time until it has touched or been played by another player. The goal kick must be played from the ground, as the laws of the game do not permit it to be played initially from the goalkeeper's hands.

The goal kick is generally taken by a fullback or the goalkeeper. During a goal kick situation, a goalkeeper will, quite often, fake a long kick and pass the ball out of the penalty area to a teammate

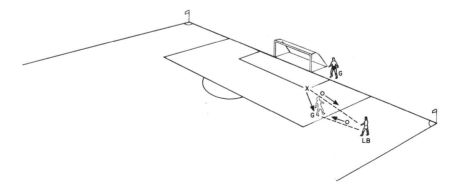

Fig. 5–24. An inter-pass play between a goalkeeper and a fullback during a goal kick situation.

who, in turn, passes it back into the penalty area to be handled by the goalkeeper for a clearance kick or throw. (See Fig. 5–24.)

Fig. 5–25 shows both teams positioned for a goal kick. Note that the left back for the kicking team is playing back to cover the front of the goal, in case of a poor goal kick. As a rule, the kick is directed to a wingman, unless the kicker has a teammate open around the middle of the field. If the kicking team is favored with a strong wind, a goal kick can be very effective when directed down the middle of the field, especially if the opponents are playing too close to the kicker.

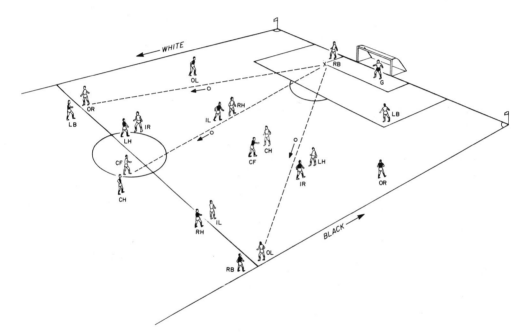

Fig. 5–25. Two teams positioned for a goal kick situation.

CORNER KICKS

When a corner kick occurs, both the defense and offense must be prepared to react immediately to the situation. For the defense, the goalkeeper and his two fullbacks take definite positions: one fullback stands close to the goal post that is nearest the corner from where the kick is to be taken; the other fullback takes a similar position near the far goal post; and the goalkeeper stands just in front of the goal line and also near the far post. The goalkeeper's position

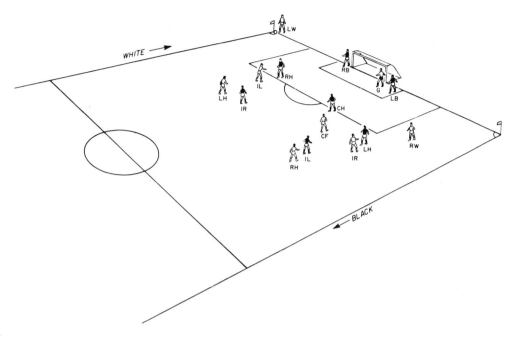

Fig. 5–26.   A corner kick situation.

affords him the best view of the flight of the ball and the movements of his opponents. From this position, he is able to move forward if necessary in order to play the ball. (See Fig. 5–26.) Generally, the goalkeeper will move out of the goal to catch or fist the ball away when it is directed into or near the goal area. When the goalkeeper leaves the goal, it is the responsibility of one or both of the fullbacks to move in to defend it until the threat of a score is averted.

The positions of other defenders vary according to the strategy of the attacking team. As a rule, defenders use man-to-man marking around every member of the attacking team who is positioned near the goal or in a position that is likely to become involved in the play. However, once the kick is taken the defenders concentrate their efforts toward playing the ball.

A corner kick presents a scoring opportunity for the attacking team. The laws of the game permit any member of the attacking team to make the corner kick; however, it is usually taken by the wingman who is positioned on the side of the field from which the corner kick is to be taken. A goal may be scored direct from such a kick. On occasion, players attempt to kick the ball directly into the goal from the corner, especially if the goalkeeper is inexperienced or if weather conditions are such that it is difficult for the goalkeeper to handle the ball. However, for best results the corner kick should be lofted to a spot in front of the goal that is just far enough away from the goalkeeper to make it dangerous for him to leave the goal to handle the ball. The ball should also be kicked high enough to clear any defenders who are likely to intercept it before it reaches the target area. Many kickers control the flight of the ball in such a manner that it can either be curved toward or away from the goal. A corner kick that is curved away from the goal is called an out-swinger while one that is curved toward the goal is called an in-swinger. As a rule, an in-swinger is easier for the goalkeeper to handle. From the standpoint of the offense, the out-swinger is more difficult for the goalkeeper to handle, and it gives attackers an opportunity to meet the ball while it is curving toward them. The result is usually better accuracy and momentum for a head shot at goal. To kick an in-swinger from the right corner of the field, use the inside of the instep of the left foot and follow through for a short distance. To kick an out-swinger from the right corner of the field, use the inside of the instep of the right foot and follow through for a short distance. To execute the same kicks from the left corner of the field, reverse the order of the kicking feet. (See Fig. 5–27.) To loft the ball into the air, use the kicking technique described in Chapter 3.

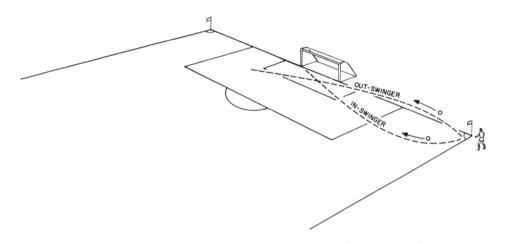

Fig. 5–27. A corner kick can be made to curve toward or away from the goal.

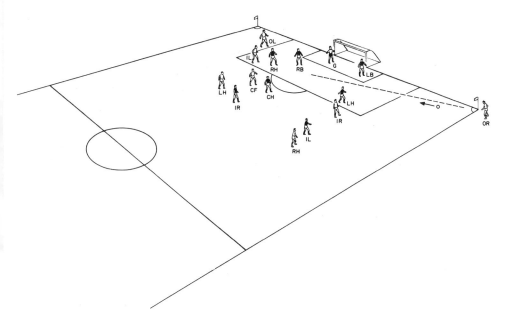

Fig. 5–28. A corner kick requires good positioning by the attacking players.

The positioning of the attackers in and around the goal area depends on the strategy to be served. Some teams position their players away from the goal in an effort to draw out the defenders. Staying out of the goal area also gives the attackers opportunities to move toward the ball when attempting to head it into the goal. (See Fig. 5–28.) Other tactics involve attackers who mill in and around the goal area. A circumstance that commonly occurs in a corner-kicking situation involves screening by players from both sides, which tends to create confusion in and around the goal.

OFF-SIDE TACTICS

The rule book specifies and interprets the various situations in a soccer game that determine whether or not a player is off-side. It is essential for players to become thoroughly acquainted with the off-side rule and to know how and when to apply it to the strategy of the game.

The off-side rule is important to defensive soccer strategy because it places certain limits on the offense. It is to the defenders' advantage to use off-side tactics immediately after the ball has been cleared from the penalty area or when the opposition is awarded a free kick inside the defenders' half of the field, providing the kick is not taken from a point on the field that is less than ten yards from the penalty area. Off-side tactics are considered to be too much of a risk when used against a free kick that is within or close to the penalty area. When using off-side tactics against a free kick, the defenders must allow for the space and advantage needed by their goalkeeper if he has to move out to play the ball. To set an off-side trap, the defenders line up laterally with the opposing forwards. If a forward breaks toward the defenders' goal before the ball has been played forward, the defenders move downfield to place the opponents in a position that is obviously off-side. This results in an off-side violation and the ball is awarded to the defenders, at the point where the off-side occurred. (See Fig. 5–29.)

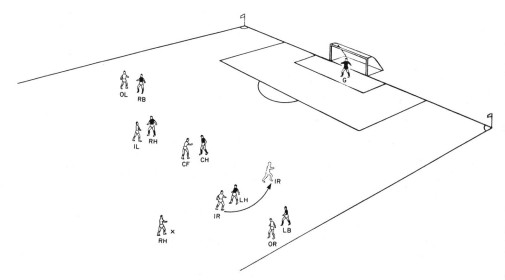

Fig. 5–29. The off-side trap.

The attacking team must be alert to possible off-side situations, and they must be prepared to take advantage of a defense that elects to use off-side tactics when it has poor field position. Too much space between the defenders and their goalkeeper often gives the opponents the opening they need for a fast-break that is timed to move with the ball. The off-side is not judged at the moment the

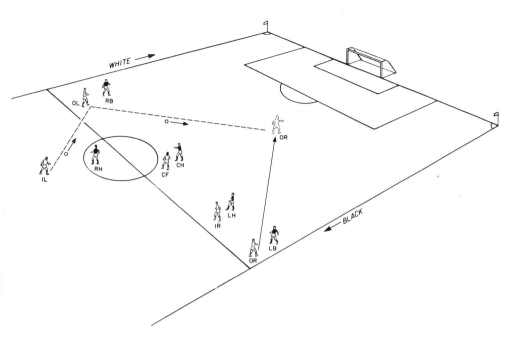

Fig. 5–30. A player does not become off-side if he goes forward during the flight of the ball.

player receives the ball but at the moment when the ball is passed to him by one of his own side. Therefore, a player who is not in an off-side position when one of his teammates passes the ball to him, or takes a free kick, does not become off-side if he goes forward during the flight of the ball. (See Fig. 5–30.)

FOUL SITUATIONS

When an infringement of a rule occurs in a soccer game, play is stopped and the ball is awarded to the offended side. Thus a foul situation has a definite bearing upon subsequent play. Quite often a game is won or lost as the result of play that stems from a rule violation. Team strategy should include offensive and defensive skills and tactics that help players react favorably to a foul situation. When planning strategy related to rule violations, consider the following situations:

For a *free kick* the ball is played from the point on the field where the infraction occurred. The laws of the game require an opponent to be at least ten yards away from the ball when a free kick is taken. When the referee awards an *indirect free kick*, he signals it by raising his arm and then blows a quick whistle for the free kick to be taken, providing the ball is stationary and at the point where the infraction occurred. A signal is not required in the case of a *direct free kick*. Quite often attackers place the ball in its proper place as fast as possible and kick it before the defenders assume their proper defensive positions. This is good strategy and should be encouraged. Of course, if an attacker elects to kick the ball without delay, he runs the risk of kicking it into an opponent who is close to the play and has not had sufficient time to move the required ten-yard distance from the ball. Under such conditions, the defender is not penalized and play continues. However, if a defender deliberately remains close to the ball, the referee will call for a replay if the ball has been kicked, and delay the game until the defense is at least 10 yards from the ball. Defenders who persistently delay a free kick are subject to dismissal from the game.

When a team is awarded a direct or indirect kick in its own side or near the middle of the field, the situation is not as critical for the defenders as it would be for a free kick near their penalty area. For situations that are not critical, defenders use tactics similar to those used against a throw-in situation. The situation becomes critical when a direct free kick is awarded at a spot near the defenders' penalty area that definitely favors the kicker and is likely to result in a score. Under such conditions, it is necessary for the defenders to form a *human wall* in front of the ball. The arrangement of the

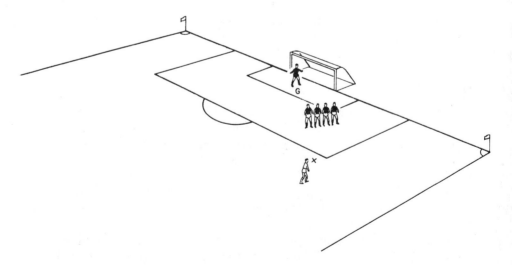

Fig. 5–31.   A human barrier against a free kick near the penalty area.

wall is directed by the goalkeeper and, as a rule, four defenders are used to form the barrier. The goalkeeper directs one of the defenders to a position on the flank of the wall that puts him in line with the near goal post and the ball, and his three teammates stand next to him in side-by-side positions. Once the barrier is formed, the goalkeeper moves closer to the far goal post to protect the exposed portion of the goal. (See Fig. 5–31.) If a human barrier is needed against a shot taken from a point that is directly in front of the goal, the goalkeeper might elect to split the four-man wall and position his defenders so that they will protect the sides of the goal while he assumes a position in the middle portion of the goal. The human wall, in either of these cases, cuts down the angle of possibility for the shooter and gives the goal the added protection it needs in a critical situation.

When a free kick that does not present a direct threat to the goal is awarded near the defenders' penalty area, the defensive positioning is similar to a corner-kick situation and the tactics involved are basically the same. In any free-kick situation, it is important for the defenders to recover to their positions as soon as possible. To apply off-side tactics to a free-kick situation, use them in the manner and under the conditions previously described in this chapter.

APPENDIXES

Appendix A

Organizations
and Activities

The following sponsoring organizations are responsible for the various outlets for soccer in the United States:

THE UNITED STATES SOCCER FOOTBALL ASSOCIATION

The USSFA was founded in 1913 and is the national governing body for both professional and amateur soccer in the United States. The USSFA is affiliated at the international level with the Federation Internationale de Football Association, a federation of over 125 nations. The USSFA joined FIFA in 1914.

Affiliated Organizations of the USSFA.

American Soccer League, Inc.
Arizona Soccer Football Association, Inc.
California Soccer Football Association
Colorado State Soccer Association
Connecticut State Soccer Football Association
Florida State Soccer Association
Football Association of Eastern Pennsylvania
Georgia Soccer Football Association
Hawaii Soccer Association
Illinois Soccer Association
Louisiana Soccer Association
Maryland State and District of Columbia Soccer Association
Michigan Soccer Football Commission
Minnesota Soccer Football Association
Missouri Soccer Federation
Nevada Soccer Football Association
New Jersey State Football Association
North Massachusetts and New Hampshire State Soccer Football Association
North Texas State Soccer Association
Northwestern New York State Football Association
Ohio–Indiana Soccer League

Ohio State Soccer Football Association
Oregon Soccer Football Association
South Texas State Soccer Association
Southern California Soccer Football Association
Southern New England Soccer Football Association
Southern New York State Soccer Football Association
Utah Soccer Football Association
Washington State Football Association
Western Pennsylvania Soccer Association
Wisconsin Soccer Association

Associate Members of the USSFA.

Amateur Athletic Union of the United States
Intercollegiate Soccer Football Association of America
National Collegiate Athletic Association
National Federation of State High School Athletic Associations
National Soccer Coaches Association of America

UNITED STATES OLYMPIC COMMITTEE

At a meeting of the United States Olympic Committee, a soccer football games committee is elected for forthcoming Olympic and/or Pan American Games. The soccer games committee includes representatives from the USSFA, the National Collegiate Athletic Association, and the United States Armed Forces.

The United States Soccer Football Committee is charged with the duty of determining the place, time, and method of holding tryouts or other competitions for the selection of members of the team for the Olympic or Pan American Games. In addition, the games committee nominates the manager and coaches, subject to the approval of the Board of Directors of the United States Olympic Committee.

INTERCOLLEGIATE SOCCER FOOTBALL ASSOCIATION

The ISFA is the intercollegiate group representing soccer. Through a rules committee appointed by the National College Athletic Association, it controls and regulates the sport for the colleges and universities of the United States. The ISFA maintains membership in the National Collegiate Athletic Association, the United States Olympic Committee, and the United States Soccer Football Association.

NATIONAL SOCCER COACHES ASSOCIATION OF AMERICA

Membership in the NSCAA is open to all soccer coaches and anyone interested in the sport. The NSCAA works closely with the ISFA and has assumed various functions that have contributed to the growth of soccer in the United States: the annual selection of an All-American Intercollegiate soccer squad; the publication of the *Soccer Journal;* and the operation of a film library, which is available to the membership.

INTERNATIONAL MILITARY SPORTS COUNCIL

The thirty-nation Conseil International du Sport Militaire (CISM), or International Military Sports Council, is a military organization dedicated to the promotion of world-wide goodwill through military sports competition. Its headquarters are in Brussels, Belgium; and its membership is world-wide.

The roots of CISM stem from the Allied Forces Sports Council, formed in Europe at American instigation at the end of World War II. The AFSC was designed to promote athletic competition among the personnel of the Allied occupation armies.

Seventeen different sports championships are sponsored by CISM. Team sports cover basketball, soccer, water polo, volleyball, and cross country. The United States Department of Defense attaches as much importance to United States military participation in CISM competition as it does to the Olympics and Pan American Games.

TOURNAMENTS AND COMPETITIONS

Under the direction and supervision of these organizations, the following competitions are available to soccer programs in the United States:

The World Cup. The World Cup is the real world series of soccer because competition is open to all the nations of the world. The World Cup is staged every four years. Usually, about seventy or more nations enter teams, thus necessitating a lengthy elimination series that sometimes takes more than a year to complete. As a rule, the organization of the World Cup Tournament calls for sixteen teams in the 1/8 Finals. Fourteen teams earn their way through zone competitions and the other two berths are awarded to the defending team and the host country.

In 1950 Uruguay defeated Brazil in Rio de Janeiro before a crowd of 199,842 people. In this same tournament, the United States stunned the world by defeating England 1–0 in one of the earlier rounds of play. In July of 1966, England defeated West Germany for the World Cup. Over 400,-000,000 people throughout the world witnessed the action over Telstar television.

The Olympic Games. Soccer football was first introduced into the Olympic Games program in 1900; however, the United States waited until the 1924 Olympics at Paris to send a team to the Games.

Usually, over seventy-five nations enter soccer teams in the qualifying rounds that lead up to the Olympic Games. As a rule, zone eliminations are held prior to the Games, and the field is reduced to fourteen teams. Also, the host country and the defending Gold Medal winner automatically qualify.

Pan American Games. Competitions are restricted to the nations of the Western Hemisphere and follow a format similar to the Olympic Games. The Pan American Games are staged every four years and are scheduled for the year just prior to the Olympic Games. The first Pan American Games were staged in 1951.

The National Collegiate Soccer Championship. The National Collegiate Soccer Championship is staged annually under the control, direction, and supervision of the NCAA Soccer Rules Committee.

The NCAA Soccer Championship was conducted for the first time in the fall of 1959 to determine a national champion among the NCAA member institutions who conducted intercollegiate soccer programs at that time.

National Challenge Cup. The National Challenge Cup is organized and administered annually by the United States Soccer Football Association. It was first played during the 1912–13 season and was offered only for amateur play. Today the tournament is open to all professional and amateur teams and the winner is considered the champion of the United States.

National Amateur Challenge Cup. The USSFA sponsored the first National Amateur Challenge Cup during the 1922–23 season. This tournament is an outlet for amateur teams to compete annually for national honors.

CISM Championship. The CISM Soccer Championship is sponsored annually by the International Military Sports Council. The competition is open to military teams from the thirty member nations.

In 1957, over 150,000 watched France defeat Argentina in the CISM Soccer Championship Game. The game was played in Buenos Aires, Argentina.

Age-Group Soccer. The majority of the organizations affiliated with the USSFA provide opportunities for Junior soccer. Since 1935 junior teams have competed for the National Junior Cup on an annual basis.

In recent years, many sections of the nation have adopted soccer as an age-group activity. In an effort to establish a stronger and broader foundation

Age-group soccer is growing throughout the United States.

for winning teams in future Olympic Games, the United States Olympic Soccer Committee, in association with the United States Soccer Football Association, the Intercollegiate Soccer Football Association, and the National Soccer Coaches Association, has instituted a nation-wide soccer football development program. The coordinated soccer football development program is bringing soccer to children in the six- to twelve-year age group, and it is also working to increase the number of secondary schools and colleges that include the sport in their programs.

Information about all phases of the United States soccer development programs may be obtained from the secretary of the United States Olympic Soccer Committee.

Professional Soccer. Professional soccer was introduced to the United States on a national scale in 1967. Nationally televised professional soccer games have been responsible for introducing sports fans of the United States to the caliber of competition that has been enjoyed by some of the major soccer powers of the world for many years. In addition, professional soccer has served as an impetus for other soccer programs throughout the United States.

Appendix B

Soccer Checklist
(Home Game)

PERSONNEL

_____	1. Referee
_____	2. Linemen
_____	3. Scorer (College Game)
_____	4. Timer (College Game)
_____	5. Announcer
_____	6. Stadium Custodian
_____	7. Ticket Sellers
_____	8. Ticket Takers
_____	9. Ushers
_____	10. Police
_____	11. Doctor or Trainer

FACILITIES

_____	1. Goals
_____	2. Nets for Goals
_____	3. Four Flag Poles (Two additional at mid-field are optional.)
_____	4. Preparation of Field
_____	5. Stadium Lights (Night Game)
_____	6. Field Clock (College Game)
_____	7. Timer's Table (College Game)
_____	8. Benches for Players
_____	9. Visitor's Dressing Room
_____	10. Equipment Room
_____	11. Press Accommodations

EQUIPMENT

_____	1. Game Ball
_____	2. Practice Balls
_____	3. Public Address System

_____ 4. Blackboard in Visiting Team Room
_____ 5. Blackboard for Home Team
_____ 6. Extra Whistle
_____ 7. Horn (College Game)
_____ 8. Gun and Blanks (College Game)
_____ 9. Towels for Visiting Team
_____ 10. First Aid Kit

PROGRAM

_____ 1. Pre-Game Ceremonies
_____ 2. Game Program
_____ 3. Music (Live or Records)
_____ 4. Team Line-Ups
_____ 5. Half-Time Program

MISCELLANEOUS

_____ 1. Score Book
_____ 2. Rule Book
_____ 3. Meet Visiting Team
_____ 4. Oranges or Hot Tea for Half Time
_____ 5. Pre-Game Publicity
_____ 6. Advance Ticket Sales

Appendix C

Administration of
Tournaments

The success of a soccer tournament is largely dependent upon how well it is planned and administered. A tournament demands a considerable amount of detailed preparation. To aid those who are responsible for conducting a tournament, the following recommendations are made:

ORGANIZATION OF TOURNAMENT COMMITTEES

When the site and date of the tournament have been definitely determined, select a tournament committee. The committee members are usually as follows: honorary chairman, tournament chairman, entertainment chairman, public relations officer, and finance and transportation officer. These men may select their own committee personnel. Members of committees, their size, and duties will vary, of course, for different tournaments.

TOURNAMENT ARRANGEMENTS AND EQUIPMENT

Have the following equipment ready for the opening of the tournament: game balls; ribbons for players, coaches, officials, committeemen, and service; trophies for team championship, runner-up awards, and special awards.

Make plans to have the field marked and ready for the opening game. Alert ushers, servicemen, and others as to their duties.

Contact the local Chamber of Commerce, service or civic organizations, theaters, and fraternal clubs to assist in providing entertainment for players and visitors. Arrange bus and taxi transportation for the convenience of the players and the coaches.

Make hotel reservations for committee members and special guests. Arrange for block reservations so that visiting teams can confirm their own reservations without inconvenience. Reserve meeting rooms for committees, coaches, and officials. Reservations for officials of the tournament should be made, if possible, apart from the players and coaches.

Upon arrival, give coaches and players copies of all information relating to the tournament. Have buses available to take coaches and players back and forth from the central headquarters to practice fields or site of tournament play, as required.

INFORMATION CIRCULARS

Mail information circulars containing news of the tournament, hotels available, avenues of transportation to game site, and other pertinent information at least one month before the opening date. At the same time, request biographical sketches and photographs of players and coaches for publicity use.

TICKET SALES AND TRANSPORTATION FINANCE

The local committee should set the price for tickets. Admission to games should be by ticket only; badges or ribbons should serve as identification. Special sections should be set aside for coaches, committee members, and players.

If teams are to be reimbursed for their transportation expense, a copy of the transportation charges for each team should be given to the transportation officer at the final morning meeting of the tournament.

After all bills against the tournament are received, a financial statement should be drawn up in accordance with a form that has been standardized for that purpose.

PUBLICITY AND PUBLIC RELATIONS

The responsibilities of a tournament publicity director are threefold. First, he must gather all the informational material necessary for the promotion of the tournament. Then, he must use this material wisely in his advance publicity campaign to build up public interest. Finally, he must follow through by providing proper accommodations and service for the press, radio, and television.

The dissatisfaction of newsmen and radio and television representatives often nullifies all previous efforts, so plan well to have accommodations and services that will permit the press, radio, and television people to perform their duties with some degree of convenience and pleasure. It will pay dividends.

PREPARATION OF INFORMATIONAL MATERIAL

Contact coaches and publicity directors of teams participating in the tournament. Request their cooperation in sending:

1. Biographical sketches of individual players and coaches.
2. Glossy photographs of individual or team action, preferably 8 × 10 in size, with suitable background.
3. Team's record in soccer, past and present seasons.
4. Periodical reports on season performances so material is up to date.

Impress upon the tournament director the importance of being fully informed immediately as to progress and development of tournament plans, appointment of committees, selection of officials, and team entries. Contact officials or publicity directors of previous tournaments for information and records that may be used either for reference or for comparison in publicity releases.

OUTLINE FOR ADVANCE PUBLICITY CAMPAIGN

1. General news stories
   a. Announcement of tournament dates, site, and participating teams.
   b. Announcement of tournament manager or game director.
   c. Appointment of local committee members.
   d. Announcement of ticket price scale and sales.
   e. Final tournament plans, special entertainment.
   f. Selection of referees.
   g. Pairings for tournament.
   h. Committee announcements.
2. Feature stories
   a. Brief biographical sketches of outstanding players.
   b. Art layouts, either pictorial or caricature.
   c. History of tournament (attendance figures, past champions).
   d. Press, radio, and television interviews (players, coaches, publicity men, tournament officials, special guests).

PRESS, RADIO, AND TELEVISION ACCOMMODATION AND SERVICE

If possible, all bona fide newspaper, radio, and television representatives actively engaged in covering the tournament should be given working seats at the soccer stadium. Accommodations should also be provided for Western Union operators if needed for running wire coverage; otherwise they can be located elsewhere and messenger service arranged for delivery of copy from the site of the games. Photographers should be permitted on the field, either along the touch lines or behind the goal line.

Prepare a booklet that contains detailed information on players, teams, rules, and other highlights pertinent to the tournament or game.

Appendix D

Clinics and Soccer Materials

CLINICS

The purpose of a soccer clinic is to provide opportunities to acquire greater knowledge and understanding of the sport. In addition, a clinic can be used to introduce the sport or as a part of an in-service training program. The following information is offered to those who have the responsibility of planning a soccer clinic:

Planning the Clinic.

1. Determine topics to be covered.
2. Select soccer experts and other knowledgeable people for clinic staff.
3. Select clinic site.
4. Select most suitable dates for clinic.
5. Select time and place for registration.
6. Suggest living accommodations for overnight stays: hotels, motels, school accommodations, etc.
7. List convenient eating establishments.
8. List current community entertainment: cultural events, recreational movies, etc.
9. Arrange for clinic facilities: field, dressing rooms, seating for participants and spectators, goals, nets, marking of field, etc.
10. Obtain equipment: soccer balls, loudspeaker and microphone for clinic instructors, registration table, audio-visual aids equipment, films, film loops, etc.
11. Materials: take-home kit of teaching materials.
12. Select non-teaching clinic personnel: guides, refreshments, registration, etc.
13. Publicity: local newspaper, radio, television, clinic brochure, flyers to soccer associations, school clubs, recreation departments, etc.
14. Contact sporting goods stores for equipment displays.
15. Determine tuition fee if clinic is credited by college or university.

Clinic Arrangements.

1. Plan registration.
2. Forms to acquire information from those in attendance.
3. Meet with clinic staff to coordinate program.
4. Assign display space to sporting goods stores.
5. Evaluation forms for clinic participants.
6. Test (for credit registrants only).

Suggested Clinic Topics.

1. "Role of Soccer in the School's Sports Program"
2. "Initiating New Soccer Programs"
3. "Lead-up Games for Soccer"
4. "Selling the Sport"
5. "Soccer Rules in a Nutshell"
6. "Organizing the Soccer Class"
7. "Soccer in Physical Education"
8. "Adapting School Facilities to Soccer Uses"
9. "Motivating New Soccer Programs"
10. "Soccer Fundamentals"
11. "Soccer and Physical Fitness"

Sample Time Schedule—One-Day Clinic.

8:30– 9:00	Registration
9:00– 9:30	"Lead-up Games for Soccer"
9:30–10:00	Laws of the Game
10:00–10:30	Adapting School Facilities to Soccer Uses
10:30–11:00	The WM Formation
11:00–12:00	Movie—"Soccer Fundamentals"
12:00– 1:00	Luncheon—Speaker: "Soccer in the Olympic Games"
1:00– 2:00	Demonstration—Soccer Fundamentals
2:00– 3:00	Officiating Demonstration
3:00– 4:00	Exhibition Game
4:00– 4:30	Evaluation of Clinic

SOCCER MATERIALS

Films, filmstrips, film loops, charts, rule books, periodicals, and books are excellent teaching aids and sources of information for teachers, coaches, and players. The majority of the United States Soccer Football Associations sponsor regional film libraries.

Colleges and universities sponsoring soccer programs are usually excellent sources for soccer materials. For names, addresses, and school affiliations of current intercollegiate soccer coaches, the reader is referred to *The Blue Book of College Athletics. The Blue Book* is published annually by McNitts, Inc., Cleveland, Ohio.

One of the services provided by the National Soccer Coaches Association of America is a film library. The films are available only to NSCAA members. Membership in the association, along with information regarding policy for ordering films, may be obtained by writing to the National Soccer Coaches Association.

1965 National Soccer Coaches Association of America Film Library Listings.[1]

The Great Game: Soccer
Features: 23 minutes—black and white—sound.
Description: explains the favorite sport of Great Britain and the popularity of the game among the children and men who seem to play the sport everywhere, in fields, schoc' yards, or streets. Shows amateurs and professionals teaching young enthusiasts and the finale of the Cup Competition in England. Promotional- and educational-type film. Desirable for junior and senior high school, college, or adult group. Copies available—two.

Soccer—The Universal Game
Features: 11 minutes—black and white—sound.
Description: intended as an introduction for Americans of all ages to the world's most widely played team sport, soccer. Demonstrates fundamentals and technique of the game by means of both action shots and animation sequences. An excellent educational film with promotional value. Copies of film—two.

Matt Busby on Soccer Fundamentals
Features: 12 minutes—800 feet—color—sound.
Description: film shows soccer great Matt Busby demonstrating soccer fundamentals with analysis and narration by Glenn Warner. Copies of film—three.

Association Soccer Part I—The Basic Skills
Features: 12 minutes—400 feet—black and white—sound.
Description: film aims to explain principles of play and their application and demonstrates fundamental skills. Part I explains the principles of running to ball, quick control, and utilizing the feint. Sequences from international matches are shown to illustrate use of skill. Copies of film—two.

Association Soccer Part II—The Basic Skills
Features: 12 minutes—400 feet—black and white—sound.
Description: has same aim as Part I; in addition, treats moving to position to receive pass, regaining possession of ball, trying to break through a defense, and shooting hard when possible. Copies of film—two.

Trapping
Features: 10 minutes—400 feet—black and white—sound.
Description: this film deals exclusively with ball control, especially trapping. It shows some of England's outstanding players: Mannion, Mortensen, and Matthews. It also shows how similar training can be carried out by high school or college players. Copies of film—one.

[1] Walter F. Ersing, *National Soccer Coaches Association* (Springfield, Massachusetts, 1965).

Methods of Coaching

Features: 10 minutes—400 feet—black and white—sound.
Description: underlines the importance of skill, stamina, and speed, and shows how players can best develop these qualities. Various skills, such as dribbling and heading, are used in emphasizing the following main points: (1) the use of the ball for training; (2) accuracy first, then speed in the performance of skills; (3) the practice of difficult as well as easy skills; (4) variation of speed to outwit an opponent. Copies of film—one.

Surrock on Soccer Fundamentals

Features: 20 minutes—color—silent.
Description: film displays demonstrations of advanced soccer skills by Larry Surrock, member of the 1952 United States Olympic Soccer Team. Skills demonstrated are kicking, trapping, shooting, dribbling, tackling, faking, and heading. Most desirable for individuals interested in analyzing advanced soccer skills. This print was filmed under the direction of Glenn F. H. Warner, Coach of Soccer, United States Naval Academy. Copies of film—four.

Basic Soccer Skills

Features: 10 minutes—300 feet—black and white—silent.
Description: film presents a series of shots on basic skills of soccer, which are executed by former All Americans at Oberlin College. The film was produced by Cliff Stevenson while coach of the Oberlin team. Copies of film—one.

Coaching in the Game

Features: 10 minutes—400 feet—black and white—sound.
Description: film demonstration of some of the methods that a coach may use to improve the combined play of a team, both in attack and defense. Material illustrated includes: W formation, cross field passing, open space, balancing the defense, defensive assignments, and select defensive situations. Excellent film for beginning or elementary skilled players at any educational level. Copies of film—one.

Soccer Fundamentals

Features: 10 minutes—300 feet—black and white—silent.
Description: film shows briefly the skills of kicking, heading, trapping, and throw-ins. Desirable for analytical purposes only. Copies of film—one.

Out of the Witches' Kitchen

Features: 50 minutes—2,000 feet—black and white—sound.
Description: film demonstrates training techniques employed by three of the leading international trainers or coaches. Systems used by England's Winterbottom, Italy's Herrara, and Brazil's national coach are illustrated in the film. The training sections are supplemented with six- to eight-minute series of outstanding international games involving Hungary and England, Barcelona and Benfica, and Germany and Brazil (Santos). Film excellent for coaches and players. Copies of film—one.

1962 NCAA Semi-Final Game Highlights

Features: 12 minutes—400 feet—black and white—silent.

Description: film shows spot action and scoring of the 1962 NCAA semifinal games involving Springfield College vs. Maryland University and St. Louis University vs. Michigan State University. Desirable for promotional purposes. Copies of film—one.

NCAA Highlights of St. Louis

Features: 45 minutes—1,700 feet—black and white—silent.

Description: highlights of NCAA games played by St. Louis University from 1959 to 1962, as well as a series of shots from the "Billiken"—Miami University regular season game in 1963 played before some 6,000 fans in the top intersectional match. NCAA games featured are: University of San Francisco vs. St. Louis University; 1959 Final with University of Bridgeport; 1961 Final with West Chester State College; 1962 Quarter Final with Michigan State University; and 1962 Final with University of Maryland. Copies of film—two.

1963 NCAA Championship Game—St. Louis University vs. U.S. Naval Academy

Features: 50 minutes—1,600 feet—black and white—one silent and two sound.

Description: films shows edited action of the 1963 NCAA game involving St. Louis and Navy. All three goals are shown from a high angle and ground cameras. Considered to be among the finest filming of the event. Copies of the film—three, one silent and two sound.

1964 NCAA Championship Game—Michigan State University vs. U.S. Naval Academy

Features: 60 minutes—2,300 feet—black and white—silent.

Description: film shows edited action of the 1964 NCAA game involving Michigan State University (0) and Navy (1). The only goal scored is shown from a high angle view. General positioning of majority of players during game is captured well in this film. Copies of film—one.

1960 European Cup Final—Real Madrid vs. Eintracht of Frankfurt

Features: 90 minutes—3,600 feet consisting of two reels of 1,800 feet each—black and white—sound.

Description: considered to be one of the most outstanding full game films ever to be photographed. The film covers the entire 90 minutes of play between two of the world's greatest teams and captures all 10 goals scored in the game. A classic in the list of international matches. Copies of the film—one.

European Cup—Benfica vs. Milan

Features: 90 minutes—3,600 feet consisting of two reels of 1,800 feet each—black and white—sound.

Description: film captures play from one of the most outstanding international matches between teams with contrasting systems of play. Outstanding players such as Rivera, Ghezzi, Altafani, and Eusebio among those pictured in action. Copy of film—one.

1962 World Cup Final—Brazil vs. Czechoslovakia

Features: 60 minutes—3,000 feet consisting of two reels of 1,500 feet each—black and white—sound.
Description: film captures one of the finest World Cup matches between teams marked by uniqueness in their style of play. Shots of individual action and team play outstanding. Copies of film—one.

1962 World Cup Semi-Final: Czechoslovakia vs. Yugoslavia

Features: 60 minutes—2,200 feet—black and white—sound.
Description: the game is considered to be among the finer spectacles of the 1962 World Cup Games. Quality of filming equals that of other Cup matches. Copies of film—one.

Manchester United vs. Kearney

Features: 60 minutes—1,200 feet—color—silent.
Description: film captures action of game played between two outstanding clubs, Manchester United and Kearney. The film can be used to observe team offensive and defensive patterns. Copies of film—two.

Legia—Dundee Match

Features: 30 minutes—700 feet—black and white—silent.
Description: film shows highlights of a game played at Ebbetts Field, Brooklyn, between Legia of Poland and Dundee of Scotland. Copies of film—one.

Glasgow Celtics vs. New York All Stars

Features: 40 minutes—800 feet—color—silent.
Description: first half of game played at Randalls Island, New York, May 1951, between Glasgow Celtics and New York All Stars. Copies of film—two.

Baltimore Rocket vs. The Swiss Boys Club of Bern

Features: 20 minutes—750 feet—black and white—silent.
Description: Highlights of exhibition game played in this country between Baltimore Rockets and The Swiss Boys Club of Bern. Film desirable for studying team offensive and defensive patterns. Copies of film—one.

Additional Film Rentals and Sales Now Available.

Soccer USA

Twenty-five minutes, 16mm, color, with sound.
Professionally produced for schools, clubs, athletic groups, and all soccer enthusiasts. Features scenes of World Cup Soccer, European and American professionals in action, collegiate and high school play. Produced by Fine Arts Productions, Soccer USA, Hollywood, California.

Soccer International Style

Twenty-six minutes, 16 mm, color, with sound.
Game filmed at Yankee Stadium, New York City, featuring Santos of Brazil and Inter-Milan of Italy. Produced by Tel Ra Productions, Inc., Philadelphia, Pennsylvania.

Glossary

AFSC—Allied Forces Sports Council.

Age-group soccer—Soccer programs organized for youngsters between the ages of six and twelve.

Angle of possibility—Angle within which a ball must travel in order to enter a goal.

Ball control—Maneuvering or maintaining possession of the ball.

Bounding board—A goal-size structure that allows for continuous repetition of kicking, passing, and ball control drills.

Captive ball—See suspended ball.

Center circle—A circle with a ten-yard radius marked at the center of the field.

Chip shot—A soft kick lofted into the air, with a back spin on the ball.

CISM—International Military Sports Council.

Clear—To kick, head, fist, or throw the ball well away from a potential scoring area.

Corner area—A quarter-circle with a radius of one yard that is marked inside the corner areas of the field.

Corner kick—A direct free kick taken from within the quarter-circle of a corner of the field by a member of the attacking team.

Direct free kick—A place kick situation in which a goal may be scored directly without touching another player.

Dribble—Technique used by a player to move and maintain control of the ball by propelling it with the feet.

Feint—A pretense of moving in one direction while actually moving in another.

First-time kick—To kick the ball without first trapping it.

Fisting—Punching the ball with one or both fists.

Flag pole—Five-foot rounded post placed in each corner of the field.

Full-volley—High clearance kick made with the ball before it hits the ground.

Goal area—A marked area in front of the goal that extends from the goal line, at a point 6 yards from each goal post, onto the field of play for a distance of 6 yards where the two lines are joined by a line drawn parallel to the goal line. The distance along this parallel line should measure 20 yards = 60 feet.

Goal kick—Method for the defenders to put the ball back into play after it completely crosses the goal line and is last touched by the attacking side. The rules call for an indirect kick after the ball has been placed within that half of the goal area nearest to where the ball crossed the goal line.

Goal line—The boundary line that marks each end of the field.

Half-volley—Kick made just as the ball bounces from the ground.

Hand ball or handling—Violation that results when a player other than a goal-keeper intentionally touches the ball with any part of the arm.

Human wall—A barrier of defenders positioned to assist the goalkeeper in his defense against a free kick near the goal.

Indirect free kick—A place kick situation in which a goal cannot be scored until the ball has been touched by another player. The referee's signal for the indirect free kick is indicated by raising one arm in the air.

Instep kick—Kick executed with the shoe-lace portion of the shoe.

In-swinger—A corner kick that is curved toward the goal.

Interval training—Theory of training that applies the physiological over-load principle by increasing the pace and number of repetitions, by decreasing the interval, or by doing both.

ISFA—Intercollegiate Soccer Football Association.

Kick board—See bounding board.

Kick-off—The indirect free kick taken at the center of the field when the game begins or is restarted after half-time, or after a goal has been scored. The side that loses the goal kicks-off during the game.

Lob—A soft kick lofted over a player's head.

Mark—To assume a defensive position near an opponent.

Muscular fatigue—Loss of the normal function of the muscles after they are subjected to prolonged or intense work, because of the accumulation of their waste products.

NCAA—National Collegiate Athletic Association.

NSCAA—National Soccer Coaches Association of America.

Off-side—A player who is nearer to his opponent's goal than the ball and who does not have at least two defenders between himself and the goal at the time the ball is played to him.

Out-of-bounds—When the ball completely crosses the goal line or touch line whether on the ground or in the air.

Out-swinger—A corner kick that is curved away from the goal.

Over-head kick—A kick that sends the ball back over the kicker's head.

Pass—To kick, head, or throw the ball to a teammate.

Passive resistance—Token or inactive opposition.

Penalty arc—An arc of a circle outside the penalty area that has a ten-yard radius from the penalty spot.

Penalty area—The marked space in front of the goal that extends from the goal line, at a point eighteen yards from each goal post, onto the field of play for a distance of eighteen yards, where the two lines are joined by a line drawn parallel to the goal line. The distance along this parallel line should measure 44 yards = 132 feet.

Penalty kick—Direct free kick taken from the penalty spot.

Penalty spot—Mark from which a penalty kick is taken, twelve yards from the mid-point of the goal line.

Pivot kick—Method of kicking when a player has to turn on the ball to kick it in the right direction.

Power training—A circuit program that includes weight training and other exercises that can contribute to the physical fitness needed for soccer.

Programming—An organizational plan that budgets the time allocated to a training program.

Punt-volley—To kick a ball as it is dropped from the hands.

Save—To prevent a goal.

Scissors kick—A kick with a scissors-like movement of the legs.

Score—When the entire ball passes into the goal, provided it is not thrown, carried, or propelled by a hand or arm of an attacking player.

Sidelines—See touch lines.

Sprint—Run at full speed.

Suspended ball—A free swinging ball used as a teaching and training aid.

Sweeper—Player who is positioned to back up the defense in case of a breakthrough by the opposition.

Switching tactics—Strategy that involves the deliberate change of positions by players.

Tackle—A technique used to take the ball away from an opponent, or force him to get rid of it at a disadvantage.

Throw-in—Method used to restart play when the ball is ruled out of play across the touch lines (sidelines).

Touch lines—The lines marking the length boundaries of the field (sidelines).

Training station—Space of sufficient size for conducting a drill or training phase of the soccer program.

Trap—Method for controlling the ball.

USSFA—United States Soccer Football Association.

Volley—A kick when the ball is off the ground.

Wingmen—Outside forwards who are positioned near the touch lines.

The World Cup Tournament—The world series of soccer, which is open to all nations of the world.

Bibliography

BUHRMANN, HANS GUNTHER. "The Status of Soccer at Colleges and Universities in the United States." Unpublished thesis, George Williams College, Chicago, 1963.

DiCLEMENTE, FRANK F. *Soccer Illustrated.* 2d Ed., New York: The Ronald Press Company, 1968. 250 pages.

ERSING, WALTER F. *National Soccer Coaches Association.* Springfield, Massachusetts, 1965.

LaPORTE, W. RALPH. *The Physical Education Curriculum.* Los Angeles: The University of Southern California Press, 1947.

LEISER, WILLIAM. "The Best Game of Them All," *San Francisco Chronicle,* March 7, 1962.

MENKE, FRANK G. *The Encyclopedia of Sports.* New York: A. S. Barnes and Company, 1960.

MOLLET, RAOUL. *Power Training.* Brussels: *CISM Magazine,* 1960.

THE NAVAL AVIATION PHYSICAL TRAINING MANUALS. *Soccer.* Annapolis, Maryland: United States Naval Institute, 1943. 182 pages.

The Official National Collegiate Athletic Association Soccer Guide. New York: National Collegiate Athletic Bureau, 1967.

UNITED STATES SOCCER FOOTBALL ASSOCIATION. *1966–67 Annual.* New York. 144 pages.

WADE, ALLEN. *The F.A. Guide to Training and Coaching.* London: William Heinemann Ltd., 1967. 260 pages.

WEINSTEIN, LEO. "The Physical Fitness Puzzle: A Call for Action." Unpublished article, Stanford, California, 1961.

WINTERBOTTOM, WALTER. *Soccer Coaching.* London: William Heinemann Ltd., 1964. 247 pages.

Index